THE BAR(
GUIDE TO

Buying and Selling

for the Small Business

Barclays Small Business Series

Series Editors: Colin Gray and John Stanworth

This new series of highly practical books aimed at new and established small businesses has been written by carefully selected authors in conjunction with the Small Business Unit of Barclays Bank. All the authors have a wide experience of the theory and, more important, the *practice* of small business, and they address the problems that are likely to be encountered by new businesses in a clear and accessible way, including examples and case studies drawn from real business situations.

These comprehensive but compact guides will help owners and managers of small businesses to acquire the skills that are essential if they are to operate successfully in times of rapid change in the business environment.

The Barclays Guide to Marketing for the Small Business
Len Rogers

The Barclays Guide to Computing for the Small Business
Khalid Aziz

The Barclays Guide to International Trade for the Small Business
John Wilson

The Barclays Guide to Financial Management for the Small Business
Peter Wilson

The Barclays Guide to Managing Staff for the Small Business
Iain Maitland

The Barclays Guide to Managing Growth in the Small Business
Colin Gray

The Barclays Guide to Franchising for the Small Business
John Stanworth and Brian Smith

The Barclays Guide to Law for the Small Business
Stephen Lloyd

The Barclays Guide to Buying and Selling for the Small Business
John S. Gammon

THE BARCLAYS GUIDE TO

Buying and Selling

for the Small Business

JOHN S. GAMMON

BARCLAYS
Published by
BLACKWELL

First published 1991

Basil Blackwell Ltd
108 Cowley Road, Oxford, OX4 1JF, UK

Basil Blackwell Inc.
3 Cambridge Center
Cambridge, Massachusetts 02142, USA

British Library Cataloguing in Publication Data

A CIP catalogue record for this book is available from
the British Library.

Library of Congress Cataloging in Publication Data

Gammon, John (John S.)
The Barclays guide to buying and selling for the small business /
John Gammon.
p. cm.—(Barclays small business series)
ISBN 0-631-17528-8:
1. Small business—Management. I. Title. II. Series.
HD62.7.G36 1991
658.7'2-dc20 90-21604 CIP

Typeset in 10½pt on 12½pt Plantin
by Hope Services (Abingdon) Ltd
Printed in Great Britain by
T. J. Press Ltd., Padstow, Cornwall

Contents

The author and publisher would like to point out that the use of the masculine pronoun is not gender specific.

Foreword

The last five years have seen a significant growth in the number of small businesses in all sectors of industry in the UK. Unfortunately they have also seen an increase in the numbers of problems encountered by those businesses. Often the problems could have been avoided with the right help and advice.

Barclays, in association with Basil Blackwell, is producing this series of guides to give that help and advice. They are comprehensive and written in a straightforward way. Each one has been written by a specialist in the field, in conjunction with Barclays Bank, and drawing on our joint expertise to ensure that the advice given is appropriate.

With the aid of these guides the businessman or woman will be better prepared to face the many challenges ahead, and, hopefully, will be better rewarded for their efforts.

George Cracknell
Director UK Business
Sector
Barclays Bank plc

I

Introduction

Outline

This chapter reviews the contents of the guide, who should read it and how it should be used. It summarizes:

- a step-by-step approach to buying
- a marketing approach to better selling
- the development of negotiating skills

Business is buying and selling

All business, however big or small, is about buying and selling and making a profit. This can mean running a factory and making products, which entails buying in raw materials or components, turning them into finished articles and organizing the selling. Another business option can mean using a workshop with machinery, which has to be bought, to provide a service. Or it can mean becoming expert at knowing how to buy highly specialized products and make them available in a hurry. One small business specializes in finding particular tools for particular jobs, such as fitting certain types of tiles, and hires those tools to its customers when they need them. Some businesses spend 70 per cent of their sales income on materials and equipment. Others buy very little, apart from the expertise and the time of individual people. All of these very different businesses are buying and selling.

Who should read this book?

'I am so busy doing the work that I do not have enough time to think about the strategy of the business. This is the one thing that worries me at the moment.'

This comment was made to me, not by a desk-bound executive of a large multi-national company in a glass and steel office block, but by the owner of a largely one-man business, employing one or two people from time to time. His 'office' was in a hut at the end of a workshop and yard on a light industrial estate. This book is for people like him and others running small businesses, who want an easy-to-use guide that saves them time, money and worry. For this reason each of the chapters that follow this introduction starts with a summary of what they are about and ends with an easy-to-find check list, for use in everyday situations. The *Guide* is for doers as much as for readers. It is a small investment that should give a continuing return to its users, helping them to make money.

How it should be used

This book is written to help business people make more money and it uses examples from many different types of business. Some of these will be directly relevant for some readers; others will not but may still give ideas that can be used. The best way to remember and apply the advice it contains is to take notes of

- any idea, method, or information that is new to you;
- any new idea that is 'sparked off' by reading the book.

Writing down what you already know or what is irrelevant to your particular business is unnecessary.

Taking your own decisions

More and more people are setting up their own businesses, many of them attracted by the prospect of taking their own decisions, instead of having to wait for someone else to tell them what to do. 'Buying and Selling' is about taking those decisions.

- What to buy and sell?
- From or to whom?
- How?

Scope of the buying chapters

Buying can take the form of

- buying outright, either with one payment, or with a series over an agreed period of time in a hire purchase type agreement;
- leasing, which usually costs more in the end but eliminates the need for a sudden big expense;
- hiring, when the need is for a facility, such as an extra van, for a short period of time.

In addition buying can cover:

- goods simply for resale, as in wholesaling and retailing;
- components and materials for use in manufacturing;
- products for use in the business, such as spares for machinery and print for advertising purposes;
- subcontracted services ranging from construction to cleaning;
- overheads such as premises, whether bought or leased;
- utilities, such as telephones, lighting and heating.

The buying decisions are arranged in series.

Deciding what you need

This prompts the question – do we need it at all? Some zero options are obvious, like the two partners in a computer business who used part of the initial bank loan to buy large and expensive cars, to impress potential customers. Unfortunately, that left too little to keep the business alive. More often zero option decisions are more difficult to decide, like a standby printing machine for a high-quality printing firm. Should they spend the money or risk losing business?

Make or buy

Sometimes a company needs to take a make or buy decision. Perhaps a small factory can make more money by buying in part made-up products, such as sub-assemblies, than by buying each separate component and assembling them itself. The best manufacturing facilities are those which keep the operation as simple and straightforward as they can. The more complex they are the greater the likelihood of cost increases.

Another question is: how much can we handle on our own? Buying more parts or products means more orders, more invoices, more time spent on storage and creating storage systems and perhaps renting or buying more storage space. In retail it may make more sense to identify the fast sellers, check and re-order them regularly but have standard replenishment orders for the other products. Alternatively, there are an increasing number of restaurants which buy in pre-cut steaks and other meat rather than handle the butchery in a kitchen with limited space.

How much should be bought in or subcontracted? Many one- or two-person businesses have had to decide whether to spend scarce capital on hiring a firm of shopfitters to fit the shop they have just rented, or do it themselves. Often those who do it themselves find it takes much longer than they thought. The opening is postponed and they miss the first few days trading.

Deciding priorities

What are the priorities? Management of time is often one of the hardest tasks confronting the small business person. How much time can reasonably be spent buying? Which is the more important – deciding between suppliers or knocking at the door of what could be your best customer? If the small business person is lucky enough to have time on his hands, perhaps it means that his customers come too easily because his goods or services are too cheap. If his days are full, then he needs an approach to time management. This will include looking for repetitive jobs that can be simplified into easy-to-use systems.

Some hire a part- or even full-time bookkeeper, but many do not. In which case it may be necessary to systematize the value added tax procedures into a routine that is easy to follow, so that orders, receipts and invoice copies are stored in a methodical manner and returns and payments sent off at the right time. By creating a routine – and not all small business people, by any means, regard VAT as a straightforward routine – this leaves more time for selling the services or products that are offered, or for buying. Eventually, the answer to this question is found by reference to the next question.

What benefits are we seeking?

Like most things in business, benefits are only meaningful when they are expressed in numerical terms, e.g. if a printer can reduce his paper purchasing costs by 50p a ream (500 sheets) and he uses 20 reams a day, in a year of 50 × 5 day weeks, he will save £2,500. Less straightforward is the following equation: Reducing VAT work by one hour a week will allow you time to

- Save £1,000 a year by finding cheaper suppliers,

or

- build better shop displays which sell more, adding say £750 to annual trading profits.

The only reason for buying anything for a business is to make money. 'Spending money (or time) to make money' is the basic idea of all business. It can be profitable to buy a product simply because it resells in a wholesalers or because it makes possible the provision of a profitable service, for example a carpet cleaning machine for a home visit carpet cleaning business.

The question must always be asked: 'What benefits are we seeking in buying A?' Benefits can be measured in money or time – which means money in the end.

Specifying needs

Some businesses get by for most of the time without writing down what they are going to buy, but sooner or later there is usually a misunderstanding. The advantages of writing down what you want are

- it makes you decide in logical sequence exactly what those wants are;
- it eliminates most of the potential misunderstandings with the supplier;
- it sets out the basic factors (e.g. quantity, quality, price, discounts, packaging, delivery) that can now or later be the subject of negotiation.

Who can supply it?

Having more potential suppliers than you need is a critical principle. If 11 people are each looking for a house to buy and there are 10 on the market, prices go up. If the reverse applies and 9 people are looking with 10 on the market, prices go down. Similarly, if you have more suppliers interested in your business than you need, you are better placed to obtain what you want; not just the right prices but other important requirements, such as credit, delivery and after-sales service.

Buy from firms who need your business

Satisfy yourself that potential suppliers really want your business. Often this means looking to firms that are either small like yours, or genuinely competitive and making positive and realistic claims about the ways in which they can offer you a better product and/or service. Frequently this means buying from local firms, who need your goodwill and preferably recommendation, so that their local trading chances are improved.

Clarify and compare terms of trade. What exactly are they offering, not just price, discount and credit but reliability of supply and service. A retailer who finds a supplier offering keen prices, and then has to keep customers waiting while he telephones that supplier to find out why his supplies are delayed and when they will eventually arrive, is not enjoying the competitive advantage he expected.

Researching suppliers

Researching potential suppliers has to be handled economically. Very few small businesses have time to make long lists of relevant suppliers from trade directories like *Yellow Pages*, but they do need to bear in mind that businesses are constantly closing while new ones are opening. No directory is ever completely up to date for this reason. Even when new, a quarter of directory entries can be inaccurate. This makes it important to find out about new firms, not necessarily from directories but from friends, other traders and local newspapers. Find room for a file with catalogues and price lists from firms you do not necessarily need now but might need in the future.

Hard as it may seem it does help to quantify what you need on an annual basis or, if that is unrealistic, over a shorter time period. Forecasts are rarely completely accurate but their great benefit, even if they are just guesstimates rather than carefully calculated week-by-week forecasts, is that they force you to think ahead and ask questions such as the following.

- How many suppliers should I use?
- How often and in what quantities should I buy from them?
- Where am I going to store it? This prompts questions like: Which is better; buying frequently in small quantities and saving storage, or buying in greater bulk and getting a better price?
- Most important, how can I use these plans to negotiate more successfully?

Use of supplier rating systems

When you have a bad experience with a supplier, it seems that there is no need to record it because it will never be forgotten. If you buy from comparatively few people, this may well be the case. On the other hand it can be very useful, especially in a small business with dozens of suppliers, to make assessments from time to time. These can be simple, such as recording in the file whether you thought they were good, bad or indifferent, or being more precise: giving a good, bad or indifferent assessment against each of the relevant supplier qualities. These might include:

- price,
- credit,
- ease of access to their sales staff (the best of suppliers is of limited value if his telephone line is busy most of the time),
- quantity and quality of their printed information,
- delivery,
- packaging – product protection,
- after-sales service – do they seem to disappear once delivery is complete and invoice paid?

Any supplier information is valuable if it strengthens your negotiating position, but a balance has to be achieved between too little to be useful and too much to be stored and read easily.

The buying processes

Even if you are buying, you still need to 'sell' yourself as a worthwhile customer. The better the initial approach, the stronger your negotiating position when you come to buy. Depending on the size and nature of your business, you may want to contact a supplier by letter, 'phone or even fax. Whatever it is, the first consideration is to convey that you know what you want. This does not necessarily mean being absolutely precise (it may be too soon for that) but it does mean conveying a sense of purpose. A letter should be on stationery that certainly does not have to be expensive but should be easy to read and uncluttered. Any telephone enquiry should be pleasant and positive.

Make a note as to how you will judge the responses, before they come in, so they can be assessed objectively. One farmer co-operative was reviewing its suppliers, so it made a standardized enquiry and then displayed a wall chart analysis of the responses at a meeting of members, so they could decide between the various sources. Alternatively, you may be lucky and have a supplier's salesman walk in the door, just when you need him!

Most people are wary of selling to customers on credit, if those customers may not be financially sound. What is recognized less often is that it can be very inconvenient to buy from a firm that is forced to cease trading, before the order has been delivered. Size is no guarantee because small subsidiaries of large parent companies have been placed in liquidation. With a small local firm, it is often possible to glean an impression of their soundness. Otherwise there are credit reference agencies or, sometimes, it is possible to talk to some of their customers or suppliers.

Supplier's costs

It can be difficult to find out what the supplier's costs are and sometimes there is not enough time to do so. However, forewarned is forearmed. The better you understand your supplier's business, the better placed are you to bargain effectively with him. If you know how much his materials cost, what sort of machinery he needs to use, how much it costs, how much labour time is needed, you can adopt a much better negotiating position. In fact buyers in some of the larger companies are trained to find out potential suppliers' costs. Suppliers often co-operate with them if they are convinced that the intention is to allow them to make a reasonable profit and prevent an excessive one.

Cautious beginnings

Just as a retailer will buy a new product in small quantities, 'to see how it goes', so it can make sense not to buy too enthusiastically from a new supplier at the beginning of a commercial relationship. Everything may look promising but it is better to make sure, beginning with a sample for testing and then small quantities for everyday use. A small car body repair shop, for example, could find itself seriously inconvenienced, if it changed to a cheaper paint supplier too suddenly and ran into difficulties with colour matching. One discontented customer can take away months of savings on a cheaper paint.

Economic purchasing quantities

Once a business has decided to continue buying from a supplier, the question of economic purchasing quantities becomes important; essentially one of getting the right balance amongst

- the cost benefits of bulk buying and less frequent deliveries; a small retailer who is preoccupied with deliveries can pay out more in wages for sales staff, to mind the shop, if he spends too much time in the stock room;
- the inconvenience of storing goods in too little space or, worse, having to rent extra space, perhaps on another site;
- committing yourself to a certain price level and then losing out when prices come down, long before stocks are exhausted;
- using available cash to best advantage.

Value analysis

Value analysis has become a technical sounding word for the commonsense approach of looking at what you are buying and asking whether you really need all the features you are being offered in a product or service. The consumer is lucky. He or she can often look up assessments of consumer products in a magazine and read an informed opinion of the value offered for each additional feature. The small business person often has to work it out on his own! Nevertheless this can frequently be done by asking questions.

Stock control

Stock control means having stock when you need it but not too much of it. Keeping stock at the right levels means, particularly in the small business,

- storing it in an organized way, with clear labelling when necessary, so that it is all kept in one place, and can be counted easily;
- keeping simple records, which match the physical quantities of stock;
- separating different batches if, for example, they have different use or sell-by dates;
- keeping it in the right conditions; fresh produce is better kept away from dampness or heat, for example.

Stock is an investment to be converted into income, or used to generate income, as soon as possible. Keeping it too long can be unwise if too much money is invested in this way.

Benefits of standardization

It follows that simplifying the range of what is kept can save time in stock control, for example tools and spares in plumbing or jobbing building. It is better to have relatively few pieces of equipment and use and replace frequently.

Measuring results

Comparing performance with promise means keeping supplier records, unless you have a very small number of suppliers, in which case memory will suffice. Using such records to improve supplier standards is important. A good supplier can be as valuable as a good customer and make it easier to earn good profits.

Buying should be done as a routine and preferably not in an emergency. Noting what you need in a simple record as you work and using the same time each week or month for checking stock and writing or telephoning orders leaves more time and energy for building effective customer relationships.

Special record books can be bought from stationers but never scorn a simple system if it suits you. Businesses providing services, and consequently needing to buy comparatively little, have often kept good buying records in a single notebook. This combined with formal orders, either specially printed or using business stationery (letterheads) is often sufficient, provided the paper is stored in the same place.

Allowing time to buy well is important. This means looking for alternative suppliers even when all the current ones are satisfactory. It is all part of making buying as routine as possible.

Strategic marketing

This book emphasizes selling but it is necessary first to understand the term 'marketing' and its relevance to selling. Selling is only part of marketing and it is useful to be able to appreciate all the aspects of marketing, so that a sensible marketing strategy can be created and thus lead to the effective selling that any business needs.

Marketing means finding out what people want and then supplying it at a profit. The important discipline is resisting the temptation to sell what you like selling before you find out who the customers are and what they want. It is the attitude of the man who thought of opening a restaurant in a London suburb, but designed his own questionnaire and called at houses in the area to ask those questions, before signing a lease on a property or making any other definite commitments. You need to bear in mind various qualities of your business:

- Strengths: What are they compared with your competition? They might, in the case of a restaurant business, include the fact that there are no other establishments of comparable quality in the area.
- Weaknesses: Which might include the lack of suitable premises or difficulty in finding a good chef who would accept pay at a level consistent with the prices that could be charged.
- Opportunities: There might on the other hand be signs of interest in the restaurant, as an alternative to restaurants a couple of miles away where parking is difficult.
- Threats: These could include the possibility of one or more local public houses following the fashion and expanding their catering facilities.

Research means picking the right questions and getting the answers, often but not necessarily by means of a written questionnaire. This could be used when talking, as in the restaurant case, to likely customers who could, for instance, include employees of local firms as well as local residents. Other enquiries should cover any likely changes in traffic such as parking, major applications for planning permission, any changes which could affect tax or business rates.

Marketing decisions

Research should clear the way for the main marketing decisions. These fall into four categories. In the restaurant example they would be as follows.

- Product: What menus, for example, and what ambience – decor, table size, seating, lighting, background music?
- Place: Exactly where should it be? Are there easily converted

premises available? Is there a choice between a main thoroughfare site, with a high rental, or a lower rental site on a side road, which would, however, need more expenditure on advertising to tell people that it was there?

- Price: At what level should prices be set? Should the aim be to have a small clientele paying high prices, for privacy and personal attention, for example?
- Promotion: This includes advertising and anything else, such as door-to-door leaflet distribution or temporary price reductions on selected menu items, designed to tell people about the restaurant and encourage customers to use it.

The remaining selling chapters (7, 8, 9 and 10) deal with these points in detail.

Selecting a range of products to sell

The following are three key questions.

- How many products should be included to give the customer the impression that a range of customer needs can be supplied, that he or she does not have to go on to a second trader to find a very similar product?
- What are the 'unique selling points' of the business and its products? How will it and they be seen and recognized as special and different by customers?
- How can the element of service be added to simple products, for example the hardware shop, where the proprietor offers solutions to do-it-yourself problems for householders, not just products?

The need for a range of services and the understanding of USPs (unique selling points) apply equally, but as services are much more subject, than products, to differing customer attitudes, it becomes particularly important to understand the customer's perceptions.

In what are theoretically single-service businesses, such perceptions are particularly significant. In practice such businesses are infrequent because what may seem a single-service business, such as furniture restoring, is in fact a range of skills applied to a variety of products. Even the self-employed bricklayer may be offering the same service to all his customers but be seen by them in many different ways. The housing construction company sees him as laying so many bricks a day. The semi-detached owner, who wants a garage built, sees him as someone who can do the most monotonous part of the job. The owner of the large period house may not notice the quality of his bricklaying, in the new extension, but will be extremely critical if the bricks he brings do not match the surrounding brickwork precisely. One company provided plastering services to builders and householders. One of its most popular practices was never to walk through a house for a job on the upstairs floors; ladders were used instead. This emphasis on cleanliness did wonders for its reputation, even though it was nothing to do with the quality of the plastering.

It is always important to know what customers think about a product or service.

Product development

The process of adding new products to a range and withdrawing old ones is continuous for many businesses. Customers and their wants are always changing.

The essence of selling is having more customers than you need, so that you do not have to compete on price. The business that can select its customers is at a great advantage.

It is important to have an idea of who you can best sell to, depending on your type of business. If this is known, then it is much easier to contact them and give them what they want. A plumber may decide he wants to mix his householder repair work with installations for house and apartment block renovators, for example. A vehicle repairer may want to specialize in certain models, in which case he needs to advertise over a wide area rather than just rely on local customers.

The simplest of products can be sold more effectively if it is sold as a service, with an element of advice; for example the jobbing printer who talks about various types of paper, instead of just offering the customer a standard product.

The self-employed sole trader needs to be aware of his own sales performance, learning from experience to create effective relationships with customers. For those who employ others to sell, leadership is important in training them to draw customers' attention to product benefits.

Product and service qualities must be clearly known and stated. This may take the form of an uncluttered and attractive shop exterior; telephoning prospects; local or trade paper advertising.

No sales approach is going to be immediately effective in every situation, and anyone who has to sell needs to develop the art of understanding why objections are made and of responding in a way that the prospective customer will sense as sympathetic to his interests.

Sales training and product knowledge will always improve sales but those who sell need an incentive that will encourage them in the inevitable situations where the sale is very close and can be achieved by that extra degree of commitment.

Keeping a customer

The best source of customers is often those who have bought already even if they have not been entirely satisfied. Any customer contact is better than none because contact is a selling opportunity.

Three customer contact techniques are particularly relevant. They do not need big money but they do need an understanding of what they are and how they can be used economically.

- Sales promotion is the process of varying the value the business offers for a product or service, with a view to gaining more regular customers. For example a gas fitter might offer cheap checks on central heating systems in the early autumn, for a limited period.
- Advertising is the simple process of telling people what the business has to offer, in a way that the business can control, for example by buying space in a local newspaper.
- Public relations means gaining important third party approval, so that they will commend the business to potential customers. Attracting the attention of local newspaper reporters by persuading them that you have a genuine news story, perhaps by arranging for a celebrity to open a new shop, for example.

Management and control

Record keeping for a small business, in addition to routine accounts, can seem like extra and unwelcome work but it is worth deciding what you want to achieve in, say, a sales promotion in terms of sales, writing it down and then comparing it with results. Leaving it to memory seldom works with sufficient precision because memory blurs with time.

Negotiating

Some business people are born dealers and enjoy it. Others are craftsmen, for example, who have to negotiate with large customers from time to time. An awareness of the main elements in negotiating is vital.

Negotiation may seem like a confrontation, but essentially it means identifying areas of mutual interest and finding a mutually acceptable compromise within them.

It is important to have a clear view before negotiating as to the most you hope to achieve and the least you are prepared to accept.

Once there is a negotiating situation under way, it usually pays to listen as much as possible. Most people like an attentive audience. On one occasion a negotiator even remained silent when the other party had finished speaking, with the result that the other party ended the silence by offering a concession!

Objections and outspoken disagreements can seem to indicate that you do not want the negotiations to proceed towards a conclusion, however well intentioned you may be. Even a simple 'why do you think that is important?' can be much more effective.

The essence of negotiating, once you have decided what you want from it, is listing everything you want and what the other side is likely to want and then asking for a concession every time you are asked to make one. Have your ammunition ready!

Often the best results in negotiation are obtained after a rehearsal with a business partner or a friend who acts as 'devil's advocate', testing you by playing the part of the other party.

Appendix

An appendix is included at the end of the book, to give

- sources of training and advice in buying and selling,
- means of auditing your own buying and selling.

Key points

- Good buying and selling are the most important ingredients of business success.
- In the right circumstances, methodical buying can add more to profits than energetic selling.
- Suppliers, markets and competitors are always changing. These changes create opportunities which should be exploited, as well as threats against which a business must take steps to protect itself.

2

Buying: Deciding what you need

Outline

The fundamental need not to spend money on the business unless it is really necessary is considered in the context of various types of business activity, including:

- retailing
- the one-man service business
- the mobile business
- buying utilities, such as energy and a telephone service
- buying print, food, building services and capital equipment

Is it necessary for the business?

The example quoted in chapter 1 of the computer software company which spent unwisely on motor cars is obvious, but other unnecessary purchases can be more difficult to spot. There is an understandable desire to buy promptly when many new businesses are established because buying is much more within the control of the business than selling. Some new business owners have been employees in larger firms, where they had to follow what seemed highly bureaucratic procedures before buying anything but the cheapest items. Released from the bureaucracy, there is a danger of buying too impetuously, which has to be resisted. Even when the case for buying a product is clear, there can still be opportunities for reducing the quantity purchased. Witness the case of the small businessman who reduced his purchases after noticing that oil drums could be sealed with 19 drops of solder rather than 20! There was an additional benefit in that soldering time per drum was reduced.

Some small businesses have started with a bank loan and this loan has been conditional on a business plan, which may have been produced in a format specified by the bank. It will probably have been designed to emphasize cash flows – the timing of payments and receipts month by month – and calculating the payments figures will have necessitated some estimating of items to be purchased and their cost. Simply including the purchases in the plan does not mean that they actually have to be bought and it is worth looking at their usefulness again. The construction of a business plan, either in specific terms on paper or in more general terms in the proprietor's mind, is a continuing process that does not end, necessarily, with either submission to the bank or the first day of trading. Planning, whether formal or informal, is designed to clarify where the business is going and how it is going to get there – essentially a continuous and ongoing process.

There is a limit to the number of purchases that can sensibly be considered in this way, at any one time, so it is best to take the most expensive first, leaving others for a later date. How many are assessed on any one occasion depends on individual circumstances.

Relating profit to buying expenditure

The critical question is: What profit will I make as a result of this expenditure? The method of working out the answer obviously varies, according to the type of business and type of expenditure.

Retailing

For example, a retailer's critical decisions include:

Premises What are the options? These might be

- a small high street location,
- a larger high street location,
- a side street location.
- two adjacent side street locations,

Deciding between these alternatives would necessitate some calculation of

- number of customers per week,
- average purchase (or transaction) value per customer,

- anticipated gross margin,
- rent or, if purchased, weekly financing cost, i.e. purchase plus interest,
- taxation (business rates).

Major product lines Relevant factors include

- likely rate of sale,
- stockholding costs, which might be ¼ per cent of purchase price per week, once payment had been made.

Shopfitting

- What impact has interior modernization had on the turnover of comparable businesses? What was the increase, if any?
- What are the costs?
- How soon will they be recovered?

The answers will depend very considerably on the type of retail business it is. A CTN (confectioner tobacconist newsagent) often relies on customers buying because they see something on display that they like. On the other hand a suburban or small town hardware store may generate much of its income by selling solutions to do-it-yourself problems, in which case expenditure on shopfitting may be unnecessary.

The one-man service firm

A one-man jobbing building business would have different decisions.

1 Can tools, ladders and materials be stored at home or in the van/truck?
2 Alternatively, will the cost of renting storage, for example a lock-up garage, be recovered in extra profits?
3 What kind of vehicle is needed?

   - Will likely customers in the area be more likely to buy his services if he uses a new or nearly new van with smart lettering on the sides?
   - Or will it make no difference if he buys a second-hand vehicle, several years old with visible wear and tear, and uses it unmarked?

The mobile business

A third type of 'Shall we spend?' situation is experienced by a mobile caterer, if the centre of its customer base, stimulated by word-of-mouth recommendation, moves steadily away from the food preparation centre. Relevant questions include the following.

- At what point is food quality adversely affected by the distance between the food preparation centre and the customer's home/premises where the food is to be served?
- How does increasing distance, between food preparation centre and customer, affect transport costs?
- What alternative locations are available?
- How would their costs affect the profitability of the business?
- Which is better: a second site or moving the whole operation to a new site?
- Can staff be recruited at the new site for food preparation?
- How much profit will the business lose if the owner – or one of the owners – has to spend time on finding and arranging the fitting out of a new site?

Customer service or manufacturing satisfaction?

This leads to a second question – how much can we handle on our own?

A business is often established because the founder has particular skills that he wishes to use for his own profit. Nevertheless, the business may develop to the point that he or she needs to consider putting less effort into making and more into selling. This affects what is bought.

The general questions to be asked are the following:

1 How many different items do we need to procure, after screening out those that are unnecessary?
2 Are there worthwhile benefits, in time or money, in seeking to reduce the number of procurement tasks?
3 If there are, how would they be reduced?

   - In a manufacturing/workshop situation, by buying part assembled products?

- By subcontracting some of the work of the business?
- By buying, from comparatively few businesses on a sale or return basis, so that precise order planning became less important – and less time consuming?

Benefit analysis

Other benefits can be obtained by good buying that are not so easily related to profitability. For example, cheap computers are used more and more by small businesses. They confer advantages of easy storage of information, which is particularly useful when space is limited. On the other hand, the instructions that accompany them are often not easy for the layman to follow and valuable time can be used up trying to apply those instructions. At present the trade-off is often between cheap but reliable equipment, with the learning disadvantage, and, on the other hand, much more expensive products, with a help facility from the manufacturers available at short notice.

Specific advantages acquired by purchasing cheap computers include

- ease of invoicing, issue of statements, credit control correspondence and other financial information;
- similar ease of order processing, progress chasing and supplier invoice verification once buying practices have been established.

Buying utilities

There can be a tendency to suspend judgement, particularly in small businesses which do not have funds for specialist consultants, when assessing costs for

- telephone and, where appropriate, fax and/or telex,
- water and sewage,
- electricity,
- gas,
- business rates.

Telephone

In the 1970s the telephone overtook the mail, in many industrial countries, as the most frequently used means of communication. It is important to have a definite view in the business as to the place of the telephone. Not all opinion is enthusiastic. One small business has a shop close to a major shopping centre, from which it operates two kinds of business:

- It sells consumer and commercial electrical and electronic products, which are towards the more sophisticated and expensive ends of their ranges. Such products include security alarms and computerized time switches.
- It offers a repair service for any electrical or electronic product, which has, however, to be brought into the shop. The small staff are extremely competent. Service is prompt and repair prices are regarded as representing good value for money.

This firm's telephone number is not listed in the telephone directory, nor made available through the telephone information services. This is deliberate because the management believes it can operate more profitably by repairing products than by answering the 'phone. Any business lost in this way is not regarded as significant.

On the other hand, many firms deliberately use telephone answering machines to improve the likelihood of callers making contact. Such equipment makes it easier for business people to handle telephone contacts when it suits them. Some answering machines have remote controllers which allow the user to call in from other locations and listen to messages. The possible benefits have to be compared with the cost of buying (or renting) the answering machine – or telephone recording machine to give it its formal title – and one additional cost. The answering machine user incurs further costs in returning calls, of which otherwise he would have been unaware.

Other telephone decisions include the following.

- How many lines are required? Will the cost of installing and renting additional lines be recovered in more business?
- How accessible does the telephone need to be? Is a cordless unit likely to be useful or will a fixed phone be adequate? Should

additional (and expensive) phones, such as portable and car phones, be provided?
- Are other telephone facilities required, such as telex and fax, or will it be sufficient to rely on local bureaux?

Water and sewage

The privatization of the remaining state-owned water companies in Great Britain has meant the imposition of more stringent requirements on the companies to provide these services. Such requirements, which are detailed and quite technical, are policed by the Office of Water Services. In the past, water and sewage charges have been set by reference to local authority rates but it is likely that this situation will change, partly because rates, for business premises, have been replaced by a nationally determined system of business rates (private householders changing to the personal tax system known as the community charge) and partly because there is not necessarily a statistical relationship between the cost of local authority services and the cost of water and sewage services. The concept of metering water is now being tested in a number of schemes and this method of charging may become more common, particularly in new buildings/ sites where meters can be installed during construction at relatively low cost.

Electricity

As electricity costs rise and the opportunities for increasing this type of energy also increase, it becomes more important to consider whether consumption can be reduced without harming the business. For example, can the lighting and heating costs of a retail store be reduced? Fortunately, the electricity companies do not exist just to maximize sales of their service. They have experienced specialists in energy conservation, who can and do advise small businesses on energy cost reduction. An enquiry to the relevant electricity company is all that is needed to start the process of consultation.

Gas

British Gas take a similar approach. Their technical consultancy service is readily available to small businesses. Any office of British Gas should be able to route an enquiry to the experts.

Business rates

It is particularly important to ensure that the business rating system has been correctly applied and that the business is not being asked to pay a rate that is significantly greater than comparable businesses. Contact should be maintained with the local Chamber of Commerce, which will be in a position to represent the interests of all small businesses in the area.

Quality

It is important to have a definite opinion of the level of quality required in a product or service. Often the best quality is not worth paying for because the business does not require it. Examples of unnecessary quality include

- stocking top price pâtés in a corner shop grocery in a dilapidated suburb;
- a graphic designer buying the best quality drawing board when he knows he can computerize within a year;
- a hardware retailer offering the highest quality, highest price tools, when much of his business comes from weekend do-it-yourself customers;
- buying a new printing machine when the owner has the knowledge and skill to find and operate a second-hand machine;
- a mobile caterer serving its meals on expensive almost exclusive crockery, to customers who are only concerned with what is on their plates.

Insufficient quality can be equally inconvenient, for example,

- the shoe repairer who cut costs by using cheaper materials – his customers found their shoes needed repairing again sooner than they expected; unfortunately, they did not tell him, they just took their custom elsewhere;

- the secretarial bureau which failed to change from dot matrix to laser printers as its customers' expectations increased.

Quality questions

If the product is being bought for resale, without alteration, and is slow to resell, two of the more likely reasons are

- it is not suited to the market,
- it has not been merchandized (i.e. presented prominently) enough.

'That product was a nuisance', was the comment of one retailer. 'I had to clear a space on the eye-level shelf to display it, but at least it went quickly once I had done that.'

If the product is being bought (cheaply) for incorporation in some other process, the saving will have been worth while if the product, in which it is included, proves satisfactory.

In a service business the cost of insufficient quality can be considerable in lost earning time. Who ever heard of a decorator boasting of buying cheaper brushes?

In such a business, the quality questions are often as follows.

- For how long do I need to be able to rely on it?
- How frequently do I need to pause for service checks?
- How much time do I need to spend on cleaning and/or maintenance?
- Is it going to be out of date before it wears out? If so, does it matter?
- What is the rough annual cost going to be, taking all these factors into account?

Specifying

Specifying what you have decided you need serves two purposes:

1 Setting out the 'shopping list' in terms of not only what you want but also

- where you want it,
- when you want it,
- for how long you want it – which can affect whether you buy, lease or hire,
- how you wish to pay for it.

2 Making it easier to plan any negotiating that may be necessary. Negotiating is essentially a matter of having a mental or written list of requirements and not conceding one without a compensatory concession by the other party.

Specifying means little without attention to particular kinds of specification. The intention here is to look at some of the buying situations more likely to be encountered by the owners of small businesses. Five have been chosen: building, print, capital equipment, maintenance and food.

Building

A frequent sign of small business prosperity is building work on their premises. Good sales performance has generated cash flowing into the business in sufficient quantities to either extend premises on available land or alter existing buildings to allow room for storage or some other purpose.

There are three particular problems associated with building work:

1 Getting value for money.
2 Ensuring that building regulations are observed and planning permission obtained when necessary. This is important not just as a matter of law abiding principle but because

   - if the rules are ignored the authorities may, if they find out, insist that the unlawful building works be removed;
   - if you own the premises and subsequently wish to dispose of them, the buyer may appoint a surveyor who discovers the omission and advises the buyer not to buy.

3 Last, not least but often forgotten: the time that you need to spend:

   - Coping with the disruption caused by the building works, sometimes even suspending trading.

- Checking that the work is being carried out as required and that proper action is taken when the unsuspected is discovered. Building is different from most other services in that builders can discover problems, such as dry rot in timber, that could not have been seen before the work began. This means you have to make an appreciation of the extra work, its cost and what difference it will make to the profitability of the business. One two-partner firm of solicitors commissioned extensive building alterations to their offices and decided that it would cause such a major distraction from their professional work that one partner was assigned to controlling the builders. The time he would require for this would deprive the partnership of thousands of pounds of fee income but was deemed necessary because the alterations were important for the development of the practice.

Taking expert advice

Just as many business people take the precaution of consulting a solicitor in appropriate circumstances, or a qualified accountant (if they do not control a limited liability company and are thus obliged to do so), so it makes sense to seek advice from a qualified architect when building work is being considered. For what will probably be a small fraction of the total cost, he or she will

- prepare drawings;
- obtain official endorsement that the proposed works are consistent with building regulations;
- obtain planning permission;
- specify the tasks to be carried out;
- prepare, or have prepared, a bill of quantities, which is simply a list of all the materials required and estimates as to how much they should cost; in building there are two prime generators of cost: the cost of materials delivered to the site and the cost of converting those materials into the building works.

This makes specifying and thus obtaining builders' estimates much easier. As a general principle, the more detailed the specification the easier it will be to assess the value of estimates. If no architect has been employed, there is the risk of getting into a general discussion about the work required.

One business was considering an extension to an existing building and called in a local builder, who quoted £*X*,000 for 'the lot'. This prompted the question: 'What is the lot?' Correspondence eventually yielded the admission that 'the lot' excluded such vital items as painting and papering the interior and supplying and laying floor coverings, which would add 20 per cent to total costs.

Building specification

A specification of building work required should include

- a general description of the work required and the facilities it is intended to make available, for example a separate food preparation room in a restaurant kitchen;
- the main dimensions, e.g. room height, length and width;
- ancillary requirements, such as plumbing, electricity and other services;
- the nature of finish required;
- drawings and quantities of materials required, if available;
- start and finish time;
- any requirements for suspending work or, for example, reducing noise, during certain trading times;
- other requirements such as maintenance of site cleanliness, restricted access for materials;
- obligation, if relevant, to accept inspection and decisions by building inspectors, for example, or environmental health officers;
- inclusion in estimates of how progress could be measured, e.g. completion of bricklaying/concreting, so that you can measure progress against the general plan and avoid anxiety about late completion.

Print

Most businesses buy print, sometimes only letterheads and other business stationery such as invoices and business cards. Others need it for in-store merchandizing, menus or price lists and other purposes. Some commission local designers, who produce artwork – on drawing boards, with typesetting machines and cameras – which is then returned to the client who commissions his own printer. Others ask the designer to find a printer. A third approach is to go direct to the printer, who makes arrangements with a designer. Two particular considerations apply in print design:

1 The need to have an overall 'house style' for the business, that is all or most of a firm's print should have a style that is particular to that firm. *This need not be expensive*. Some small firms use a particular typeface. Others have their own symbols. When a firm is first established, it is important to choose a house style, after giving careful thought to the impression the firm is trying to create amongst those with whom it trades or seeks to trade. Usually, it is sufficient to tell the designer something about the business, how you see its good points and the benefits it will generate for customers. The designer can then be left to produce his or her own ideas. When these are produced, it is important that you feel comfortable with them – they will be the basis of your selling efforts.
2 The second is the detailed design of the individual item. It is essential that it be practical, as anyone who has tried to fill in a form, with only a couple of inches on a line for his address, will know.

Specifying print

A check-list for specifying print can include

- quantity;
- item description: paper size, number of pages, colours;
- type of paper, expressed as grams per square metre; this depends in part on the amount of handling the paper will have – the longer and more frequent the period of use, the heavier the paper needs to be;
- the finish of the paper – if the product the business is selling is of apparent good quality, then a smooth finish paper may help sell it;
- copies of artwork, which can be arranged separately or by the printer;
- the type of binding, if relevant;
- proofing arrangements, to check that the article coming from the print run is consistent with specification;
- completion date and delivery requirements.

Capital equipment

Capital equipment is defined as equipment which is used repeatedly in a business and which is entered in the accounts as assets, which are written off over a period of time. Quite often it is leased rather than bought outright, to save a sudden outflow of cash. Following modern accountancy attitudes, where the recommendation is often to write off the small assets on purchase, such as typewriters, capital equipment is viewed in this section as major purchases, such as manufacturing equipment, which require particularly careful consideration before any commitment to buy. Examples include

- new tables and chairs for a restaurant, as part of an internal 'face-lift',
- a computerized typesetting machine for a print designer,
- paint spraying equipment for a vehicle repairer,
- a photocopier for a high street printshop.

Large businesses are able to employ people, often accountants, who have the time to make precise estimates of the impact of new capital equipment on the profitability of the business. In the case of a small business, it usually helps to match the business person's knowledge of what he needs with a suitably experienced accountant's skill in forecasting cash flows over a period of years. If the financial analysis is carried out thoroughly, it will prompt questions as to why each feature of the proposed equipment is necessary and thus what the specification should be. So you are likely to make a better decision if you work through the figures with an accountant. Specifying major capital items demands as much financial as technical specifying skill.

Maintenance

Planned maintenance

There is a temptation in small businesses, particularly when money is short, to postpone arrangements for planned maintenance of equipment because it is difficult to quantify benefits. Unfortunately, it is more likely to mean quantifying losses if it breaks down.

Examples include power tools used by an interior decorator, or refrigeration used by a butcher who relies on it for sales of frozen meat.

Maintenance contracts

Expenditure on maintenance contracts is a form of insurance and needs to be seen as a similar form of business expense. A maintenance contract is essentially an agreement whereby another person or firm agrees to keep specified equipment operating within specified periods of notice of breakdown. The service usually includes regular checks and where necessary repairs and replacement of defective parts, in order to minimize the occurrence of emergency call-outs. Factors to take into account include

- the ability of the user to make his own 'keep it going' repairs,
- the likely loss of profits if it does break down,
- the cost of the contract,
- the consequences of any loss of reputation for reliability, in the event of breakdown.

In specifying requirements for a maintenance contract, the following are relevant:

- Timing of serviceability checks.
- Speed of response to emergency call-outs, e.g. two-hour response.
- Supply of spares on a sale or buy-back basis. This involves keeping some essential spares on the same site as the machine, on the understanding that they will be bought back by the maintenance contractor if not used within a specific period of time.
- Length of contract.
- Cost.
- Ease of access to the servicing facility. A telephone line that is frequently busy is of no advantage.

Food

The buying of food that is preserved by processes like canning or freezing is comparatively straightforward because there is usually a consistency of product, often sustained by branding. The supplier of such produce, or products, has to be consistent if he is to sustain an adequate reputation and recover his investment in equipment.

Fresh produce has its own problems, even though there is a steady movement towards uniformity. In some small businesses, such as restaurants and mobile food shops, the chef or the owner does his own buying and there is no problem for 90 per cent of the time. If the business is expanding and there is less time for buying, or if the regular buyer is ill or absent from the business for some other reason, then specification becomes much more important. It is quite a common practice, in such circumstances, to ask the regular suppliers to select produce, but this method is inevitably more risky. Suppliers' understanding of what is wanted may be vague in critical areas, simply because the regular buyer never needed to say exactly what he wanted. Suppliers are also preoccupied with other buyers who, simply by their presence, distract the supplier. Fresh produce specifications can include such factors as

- size, perhaps expressed by a classification system, as is the case with some fruit products;
- colour and consistency of colour;
- absence of blemishes, bruising and split skin because the produce is overripe;
- cleanliness.

Meat

Fresh meat is the hardest produce to buy to a consistent standard because of the following factors.

- In some animals it is difficult to achieve consistency of carcase size, proportions, fat and lean content, without precise breeding and feeding. This is not necessarily worth while for the producer.
- The meat industry is only viable if the whole carcase is sold in some form or another. This fact of life has resulted in the essential skill of butchery – wholesale (slaughtering) and retail: using judgement and skill to separate the parts of the carcases so as to make as much money as possible out of each part. Easy grading systems, like size grading in brussels sprouts, are not practical.

Nevertheless some aspects of meat can be specified, such as

- maximum fat width,
- minimum lean proportion,
- colour.

Fortunately, consumer satisfaction with meat does not depend too much on taste. Appearance and texture, including moisture content, are more important. Therefore, difficulties in buying such produce can be overcome in the kitchen, which is relevant in restaurant businesses but less so in retailing.

Contracts

There are often opportunities to choose the type of contract that is made. Depending on circumstances these types can be as follows:

- Blanket: whereby goods or services are specified and quantified in total but only 'called off' against the contract in specific quantities, when required. This simplifies the whole process of agreeing what is to be bought. As and when the total on the contract has been supplied, a new contract may be considered.
- Long term: whereby prices and periodic supplies are agreed within the framework of a total quantity over a fixed period of time. The seller offers guaranteed prices in return for a larger volume of assured sales.
- Extended credit: whereby extra time for payment is offered in return for some other benefit for the seller, such as a better price.

Key points

- Examine buying possibilities in the context of the profit they will generate.
- Spend on maintenance to increase profits.
- Buy at the level of quality the situation demands.
- Specifying exactly what is needed is time well spent.

3

Buying: Who can supply it?

> **Outline**
>
> The search for suppliers includes:
>
> - deciding how many are required for each type of product or service
> - determining commercial requirements, such as service levels, sales support, etc.
> - using information sources effectively

Forewarned is forearmed

In any trading situation it is useful, if not invaluable, to have more potential suppliers and customers than you need to run a profitable business. The ability to go elsewhere, if a supplier becomes too expensive or unsatisfactory in other respects, such as delivering late, only delivering part orders or supplying too many products which are rejected after inspection, is essential. The alternative can be lost sales, because the products are not there to sell, or lost time spent arguing with the supplier or trying to find another supplier in a hurry. Also avoiding reliance on too few suppliers makes it less likely that they will be able to exert pressure on your costs by raising prices to you.

Some firms make a very deliberate policy of avoiding an excessive degree of dependence, to the point that they will choose to forgo opportunities in sales, or even in cost reduction, rather than abandon it. Instead they will give first priority to finding that additional supplier because they believe that by doing so the benefits will last much longer.

The pure trader, who buys and sells at what he judges to be the best times, sometimes without having to store the goods at all, is applying principles which apply to any business. Many firms, as they grow, lose sight of this fundamental fact of commercial life. They become institutions staffed by specialists, who may become efficient sales people, buyers or accountants but are not traders. Sometimes, but not often, the chief executive is a trader. More likely he too will become preoccupied with the detail of his job: attending meetings, appointing executives and visiting factories.

The potential strength of the small business is that it has much less chance of being inhibited by size and thus less chance of forgetting what trading is like.

However, there are businesses, for example in retailing, which deliberately buy most of their supplies from a single wholesaler. In return for the bulk of their custom, they are offered more attractive discounts and assistance with promotions and merchandizing. Even they will have secondary sources of supply, to supplement the main product range and allow alternative sources in an emergency, such as an unexpected demand for certain products which leaves them short. The existence of other sources gives them reassurance and leverage in buying and negotiating.

The logic of planning applies to choosing suppliers. Forewarned is forearmed. Logical planning also means methodical record keeping, records that are easy to read and use and easy to retrieve from wherever they have been stored.

Dangerous habits

In specifying the suppliers there are two dangerous but very human habits to avoid:

1 The danger of relying too much on people you know well and like. While effective business relationships are often socially congenial, not all of them are. Quite often the best deals are made with comparative strangers who nevertheless prove reliable. The goal is always an adequate number of satisfactory suppliers.
2 Deciding too soon that you have enough suppliers listed and then discovering that more research is needed. It is better to take 'one

bite of the cherry' rather than two. Having excellent knowledge of supply souces in a particular trade does not show up on the assets side of a balance sheet but it is still very useful.

Types of suppliers

Different suppliers have different approaches to business. Some are very conservative, staying with a product list that does not change much from year to year, except when *their* suppliers change their products. These conservative suppliers rely on price changes rather than new products to keep the cash flowing into their business. While such suppliers may not have a good long-term future in business, they can be a valuable support for quite a time. The conservatism that makes them reluctant to innovate can also make them good trading partners in other senses. Their people do not change very often and this makes them easier to deal with. In practice they can often offer a good service because their people know their customers and offer a steadiness and reliability of service.

On the other hand, change is at the heart of most business situations. Given an economic system that encourages individuals to set up new businesses, at very little cost, there are great incentives to think up and exploit new ideas for products and services, new ways of distributing them and making them available, or just cheaper ways of making what is already on the market. This system means opportunities for traders who know their potential suppliers and look out for the new ones. Every business needs to know conservative suppliers and innovators.

Having a supplier policy

How many potential suppliers do you need? This cannot be defined in precise terms according to the type and size of business and has to be a matter of judgement. However, the initial aim, when researching possible suppliers, should be to have two reserve suppliers, who will not be needed immediately, for each type of product. For example, a word-processing bureau will probably have two active suppliers of computer disks but be aware of two others who could be used if need be.

How to keep up to date is the next most important question. The best plan is to have a regular review of suppliers, say every six months, to decide which parts of the business might usefully have more suppliers on the reserve list. In such circumstances, there are two questions to ask:

- Which parts of the business are short of reserve suppliers?
- How big should they be?

In terms of size, there are two categories of supplier. First there are those whose size is such that the custom of even a small business is important to them. Often these will be local suppliers who know that a bad reputation with a local customer can rebound to their disadvantage. Those who have dealt with a small supplier who moves to a different area have often found, on trying to maintain the trading relationship, that the previous atmosphere of commitment had not survived the move.

The second is the much larger firm that is necessary because it has an ability to supply, sometimes at short notice, a very wide range of products. An example is the mobile car mechanic, who specializes in one make and therefore has his main account with a dealer for that make.

Potential advantages for the supplier

Looking at the possible trading relationship from the seller's point of view is helpful. What does he expect to gain, apart from the simple increase in turnover and the profits that go with it? Other advantages might be

- an additional delivery point which will make his transport system more economic;
- additional sales of some of his less popular products, thus making better use of his storage and sales administrative systems;
- enhancing his reputation in the area of your business, so that hopefully your competitors will be more likely to want to trade with him;

- a customer who may be interested in new products that he does not presently supply.

Listing requirements

A list should be made of what is required from each type of supplier. In addition to price, such a list might include

- order size discounts, which might make it better to buy larger consignments but less frequently;
- a willingness to supply very small quantities at a time;
- rebates on total volume of business within a time period, say one year; this would mean agreeing a fixed quantity of purchases, or value, which when exceeded would result in a repayment of a small percentage of what had been paid so far;
- any provision for emergency short notice delivery;
- timing of deliveries – on which days of the week can they be made? How early or how late in the day? Weekends?
- system for informing customers of changes in products and services;
- stated availability of technical support if relevant – how accessible do they say they are?
- ease of order placing and availability of their sales staff;
- system for advising of non-availability of goods; it can be extremely inconvenient to send an order through to a supplier, whose delivery arrives exactly when expected but proves to be short, without warning, of some of the items ordered;
- stated lead time from order to delivery, bearing in mind that an eager lightning-quick delivery service may mean the supplier is seriously short of business and may therefore be an unstable source of supplies;
- the full range of products and/or services; even though many of them may not be required immediately, the information may be useful on some future occasion;
- credit – how much do they offer to what size of business and for how long?
- specification, which may include
  size
  brand

colour
dimensions
technical capabilities, e.g. printing speed
protection (packaging)

Supplier survival

In some cases there is no need to buy from a firm with long-term business prospects. For example, a firm needing workshop premises does not need to worry about the survivability of each commercial property agent it contacts, as long as it does not make any payments direct to them.

On the other hand, the survivability of a building contractor is vital. An independent school contracted with a construction company to build a new hall. The contract was fairly simple in that furnishing and decorative finish were excluded. As the work proceeded, it began to fall behind schedule and the client noticed that management of the project consisted simply of visits from time to time by the construction company owner, who asked to be told of any problems and then resolved them. The client was perturbed to notice that weekly site meetings to review progress against plan were never held. Eventually, there were serious doubts as to whether the hall would be ready for major events that had already been announced. The contract was terminated, with payment for work actually done, as certified by the client's architect, and a new contractor was brought in to finish the job. Less than a year later the original contractor went bankrupt. One of the reasons was habitual overruns on contracts, which meant either that the contract was terminated early, with less revenue to cover wages and overheads, or that profit margins disappeared in an industry noted for slender margins. Had more enquiries been made about the ability of the firm to manage its business – and thus stay in business – the difficulties experienced during the project might have been avoided. Within a few years, significant defects in the building became apparent but the client had no recourse.

However, a supplier of essential raw materials may be required indefinitely, for example a supplier of special steels used in a machining process by a small workshop.

Supplier development

Once a relationship has been established with a supplier, the concept of supplier development will become important. This means looking for opportunities to improve the benefits that both parties derive from the relationship. Often many small businesses derive their strongest support from reliable and well-known suppliers. It can be useful to know that, in large firms, relations between buyers and the suppliers are often more harmonious than between the buyers and some of their colleagues. Suppliers can help or hinder and can be managed towards helping.

Researching suppliers

Researching suppliers is like any other form of research, deciding what questions to ask and to whom they should be addressed.

The preceding sections of this chapter indicate the questions. The answers can be sought from the following sources.

- Acquaintances, remembering that acquaintances will fall into two categories:

  those who can supply information themselves and
  those who know others who can supply it.

  There is more than a little truth in the old saying that 'who you know' is as important as 'what you know'. The first leads to the second. Many small business owners have found one of their greatest sources of support comes from other small business owners who, while not in competing businesses, nevertheless have a lot of knowledge that is relevant.
- Professional advisers, provided they do not charge you too much for their time! Accountants often have a wide knowledge of business, particularly the one- or two-partner practices.
- Trade journals – even when a business is still at the planning stage, perhaps with premises still to be acquired, it is worth buying the main supplier trade journals. Apart from the information they contain, they often give a 'feel' for the trade and how to operate profitably in it.

- Other works of reference, such as trade directories. Many of these are to be found in the reference sections of public libraries. Some are in college and polytechnic libraries, which are usually open to members of the public who wish to use them for reference and not as borrowers. Standard works of reference include *Kelly's Merchants Directory* (in the UK), *Kompass*, *Yellow Pages* telephone directories – which classify trades very precisely. Most people setting up or running small businesses are doers rather than readers and are not frequent visitors to libraries. The best plan is usually to tell the reference librarian what is required and use his or her expertise to find the answers. The librarian may suggest specialist directories in the library, or suggest other libraries.
- Chambers of Commerce, particularly the large city chambers, which not only have works of reference but also staff who are expert in using them.
- Company records, kept in the UK for example by Companies House, in Cardiff, with microfiche copies in London at Companies House in the City.
- Industry-wide financial analyses, maintained by companies such as Datastream.
- Credit ratings, maintained by such organizations as Dun and Bradstreet. These are available to subscribers and tend to show the average credit presently given to them by their suppliers. This indicates the soundness of the business.

Free information is often the best

The last two items, particularly, in the previous section cost money. In the event of a major purchase, that may make the expenditure worth while. There are firms that will carry out searches of company information, but even using such sources tends to be a highly specialized skill. A layman can pay a few pounds to an agency and find the results meaningless. For example, one businessman obtained information on a small manufacturing company's accounts, which showed sales volume, in a firm with 60 employees, of less than £10,000. A search was made of Companies House records and two subsidiaries were identified. Unfortunately, their records did not provide much information either.

Printed records should not be treated as completely authoritative.

Entries are subject to error and can go out of date quickly. The value of directories and the like is that they serve to eliminate the less worthwhile candidates.

Key points

- Aim to have more potential suppliers than you need. That way you are less likely to be subject to cost pressures from them.
- Do not rely too much on acquaintances for supplies.
- Some suppliers are conservative and reliable. Others can be better at offering new products and services.
- Only buy from suppliers who are likely to stay in business as long as you need them.
- Try and achieve a balance of interests, whereby supplier and customer have an equal need of each other.

4

Buying: How do you buy?

Outline

This chapter deals more with the actual detail of buying. It includes:

- making effective approaches to suppliers
- assessing their responses
- deciding from whom to buy
- keeping adequate records, so that supplier performance can be assessed
- a summary of English law as it affects buying

Initial approaches

You now have short lists of suppliers for each type of product and wish to test that list against the market. There are four main methods of approach:

Letter
Telex
Fax (facsimile transmission)
Telephone

Letters

Letters, or requests for quotations or proposals, have advantages and disadvantages.

Advantages

- They impose on the sender the discipline of setting out his requirements in a form that makes it easy to check before it is sent out.

- The copy serves as a record which makes it easy to follow up.
- Everyone has easy access to the postal system.
- It is a cheap method of transmission.
- It is the simplest of inputs into the recipient's own business.

Disadvantages

- Letters compete for attention with an increasing volume of mail, much of it direct mail shots designed to sell. In smaller businesses, mail can be put aside or even discarded because its appearance is interpreted as intended to sell.
- A response cannot be expected for several days, sometimes much longer if a detailed proposal is required.
- Some small businesses only operate on the telephone, dealing with an entire transaction on a word-of-mouth basis, not even invoicing.
- The sender has no control over the recipient's response because he is not there to influence it.

Telex

Advantages

- It demands attention by its very urgency. Larger firms are often organized to respond more quickly to telex.
- As with letters, both sides have a written record, to serve as a working paper.
- Transmission speed is of course very much faster than letter post.

Disadvantages

- It is more expensive than letters.
- Few small businesses, unless they are international traders, can justify the cost. Therefore they have to use a local bureau, which means either finding time to visit it or telephoning the message through, which generates more cost and risks misinterpretation by the bureau, who may be unfamiliar with the language of the particular business.
- The popularity of telex is being challenged by fax. Some firms have disposed of their telex machines and converted to fax.

Fax

Advantages

- Speed.
- Ease of use. Modern fax machines often incorporate a telephone, for normal speech use, and can fit on to a desk or table.

Disadvantages

- Cost – although this is declining steadily, it will continue to be much more expensive than the mail for a long time. Costs include: the machine itself; the chemically treated paper and other consumables; the cost of telephone time. If fax traffic is substantial, an additional phone line may be advisable.
- Variable reliability. Connecting one fax machine to another can sometimes take a while to achieve.
- Fax is increasingly used as a means of transmitting sales promotion literature and a purchasing enquiry can be delayed by the sheer volume of traffic.

Telephone

Advantages

- The ease of use of the modern telephone, with loudspeaking units, for example, to enable the user to refer to catalogues and other literature as he talks to suppliers.
- The low cost of units. For example a multi-function model has seen a price decrease of 80 per cent in 6 years.
- The opportunity to exert control over the relationship with the other party as it develops.

Disadvantages

- Higher cost than mail.
- The time taken in using it. It can take five or six attempts to contact the right person.
- The need to take and file notes on any conversation of importance, to reduce the risk of misunderstanding.

Reluctant suppliers

Contrary to the assumption that many people make, suppliers do not always make it easy for potential customers to find out what they have to offer. There are various reasons for this:

- They may have plenty of business already and be reluctant to spend money on increasing their supply capability. One small company has a range of office stationery that has significant advantages over competition, achieved mainly by design. There is little publicity material but sales are so buoyant that the normal incentives to customer service do not apply. Customers are sometimes so keen to buy that they travel considerable distances to collect, rather than order by mail or through distributors. Telephoned and written orders can sometimes be neglected for weeks.
- They may have a poorly organized sales office, with no one in charge to see that enquiries are processed promptly. This can occur when wages are uncompetitive and staff turnover is very high. One company set up a new branch in a new part of the country. Wages were unattractive and half the non-managerial staff had left within a month of opening.
- Their staff may have had too little training in their own products and how they should be sold. Many of the larger firms concentrate on installing computerized stock control and sales supply systems at the expense of giving their staff product information.

Impressing suppliers

The potential customer therefore needs to make a positive impact on the supplier so that he is remembered and treated as a useful source of income. This can be achieved in various ways.

- Demonstrate that you are clear in your own mind as to what you want. Even if you need to ask questions before being precise, a sense of purpose will leave its own impression.
- Work to a methodical timetable. If deadlines are used and mentioned, they can help to convey urgency and command attention.
- Take account of supplier comments and suggestions.

- Present written material on stationery that is not necessarily expensive but does stand out from other correspondence by its use of design and quality of paper. Colour can help but is not essential because modern design techniques and typesetting machinery can produce effective and eye-catching results.
- It is of course an opportunity to make it widely known that you are in business and a potential customer. Word of mouth is nearly always useful for a small business. A customer of the supplier may ask for information on businesses like your own and the supplier's recommendation can be useful, particularly if your business is comparatively new.

Preparing to approach suppliers

The preparation for approaching potential suppliers should therefore take the form of

- notes, if telephone is to be used, or
- letter, or
- request for quotation.

Whichever of the three is used the content should be similar.

1 A clear heading. It is important to ensure that the potential supplier realizes immediately that it is a request for information and not an order. Otherwise there is a risk that the buyer hears nothing until the goods arrive on his doorstep. The heading should therefore be

- request for quotation, or
- request for information.

2 Introduction – reason for writing (or telephoning). For example:

We are writing because we are interested in buying *a*, *b* and *c* from you/using your services for *x*, *y* and *z*. Before making any commitment, we would welcome information on the following points.

3 Further details of likely requirements, which can include

- quantity, over what period of time;
- individual order size;

- frequency of ordering;
- detailed description of goods or services, with technical data if appropriate such as BSI (British Standards Institution), European Community or ISO (International Standards Organization) references.
- date by which reply requested (as soon as possible should not be used; 'possible' can be a very long time away).

4 Details of information required has been mentioned earlier but can include

- price;
- discounts for quantity;
- rebates;
- normal credit facilities;
- whether credit references required;
- whether any minimum order level;
- lead time between ordering and delivery/supply and whether it varies between products/services;
- cash and carry facility, if relevant – opening times and days;
- precision with which delivery can be forecast;
- availability of blanket contract facilities, whereby detailed orders are called off against a single order, spread over a period of time;
- ordering procedures, including names of order processing staff, telephone/fax/telex numbers, address if separate, days and times when ordering facility available, whether answering machine facility available;
- whether sales representatives are available and, if so, how they can be contacted, how frequently they can call;
- availability of technical support, where appropriate, for assistance in using or adjusting products.

Organizing information

Each telephone call needs detailed notes otherwise you will finish your calls to find that the information you have varies from supplier to supplier and is difficult to compare. Some buyers find it easier to split their supplier contacting between telephone and postal communication. A sample of telephone calls, perhaps to some of the more important suppliers, gives them a better 'feel' for the job.

Standard letters

Using standard letters can simplify the task and save time. Such letters are designed with spaces to write in the information that varies with each letter but saves the trouble of starting each letter afresh. Photocopies can be taken of the standard letter and the details are handwritten in. Some large firms use this approach with their 'Request for Quotation' documents. Those using word processors can save time by setting up the letter in its standard format, copying it on to disk as many times as they need copies and then adding the individual finish to each one.

Responses over the telephone should be noted and written replies collected until the reply date.

Once the nominated reply date has been reached, those not replying to correspondence should be contacted by phone. It is important to avoid the temptation of assuming that the first potential supplier for each type of product to respond will be satisfactory. It may be that he is short of customers, or new and inexperienced in the business.

Reasons for non-reply may be purely temporary, such as

- factory shut down for two or three weeks;
- staff illness;
- correspondence not delivered by postal services.

First decisions

On the basis of these telephone calls, decisions can be made as to whether the enquiry should be pursued. Reasons for abandoning an enquiry can include

- supplier obviously not interested;
- supplier closed;
- supplier moved to an inconvenient location.

Once information has been collected from late replying suppliers, short lists can be drawn up from those that are left. This is better done on paper (or computer) with a separate sheet (or computer file) for each type of product or service, such sheets being based on the original enquiry letter. Each item on that letter is listed at the side and there should be a separate column for each supplier. This method is quicker than it seems. Not only does it guarantee a check that everything is included, but the simple act of writing it down impresses the information on the mind, so that once each section is completed you have made many of the decisions as to how much to order, from whom, remembering that the first target is to have much more interested suppliers than you need. If this is achieved you have a much better chance of controlling price and other requirements.

Judgement should have the last word

No system can automatically provide all the answers, nor should it. Judgement must have the last word but it should be the last word and not the first. In forming that judgement, help from other non-competitive businesses, either because they are local or because they are owned or managed by friends, can be useful.

Information on the surviving suppliers can now form the basis of permanent supplier records. Achieving a sensible balance between detailed control and a too casual approach is the formula for such records. The only test that matters is whether it enables the business person to control the relationship with suppliers. People differ of course. Some have exceptional memories and need comparatively few reminders – although they have to provide for the day when they are unwell and someone else has to run the business for them. Others accept that they do not remember very much but are very quick at picking up written information.

Small business record keeping

Increasingly, small businesses keep records in two parts:

1 A file for each supplier with documents, catalogues, specifications, etc.

2 Computer records, which form a bought ledger to provide easily read summaries of buying costs. Detail usually depends on the software used, which is not expensive (enthusiasts may write their own programs but most small business people have neither the time nor the inclination). That detail will usually include

- date of purchase,
- payment date if relevant,
- goods/services bought,
- cost.

Benefiting from visiting representatives

Where suppliers on the short list have representatives, they should be asked to call. Alternatively, if no representative is available and orders are likely to be large or frequent enough, it may be worth visiting the supplier. Once face-to-face contact has been made, other matters can be raised.

- Likelihood of part deliveries.
- Level of activity in the business.
- Nature of any trouble-shooting/technical support facility.
- The thoroughness or otherwise of their order processing, stock control, storage and invoicing procedures. Well thought-out systems can indicate an attention to detail that will probably generate financial stability.
- The presentation of their product information. If listing is clear and up to date, this can be another indication of a well managed activity.
- Their organization – are their people confident experts or jacks of all trades rushing around trying to get everything done?
- Information on their financial status that has not been previously gathered.

Becoming more expert

Any business person with a new business will probably be more expert in buying some goods or services than others, but by having a clear view of your own interests you can become an all-round expert. Any contact with a potential supplier's representative should be prepared, so that you can acquire information and experience of buying techniques. The object is to cover as much ground as possible at each and every meeting and make effective use of the time. This is best achieved by a check-list. That check-list should show a clear understanding of your interests and make it easy to invite the supplier, whether represented by a sales person or not, to show how he can advance those interests.

Suppliers who are worth visiting, but do not have sales representatives, should be asked to spare a specified period of time because 'your business may be important to us'. If a business seems unmoved by this implied compliment, it may mean that they are too inactive to exert themselves on a customer's behalf – a danger sign for any buyer.

On leaving any supplier who seems to be potentially useful, it is important to leave the impression that the visit has been worth while and that

- you have a clear view as to what has been achieved;
- you have told them what you intend to do next.

Alternatively, if it seems unlikely that they will be useful in the near future, they should simply be thanked and told that you will be in touch if you decide to order.

Collecting supplier cost information

There is an aspect of supplier visits which can be exploited if the climate is right, and that is obtaining information on supplier costs. In some large companies the buyer is expected, as a matter of routine, to identify the cost of each major contributor to supplier cost. The information is then used in negotiation but usually when the buyer is seeking to build a long-term relationship, with reasonable profits for the supplier, not to knock the price down to a level where the purchase is just a short-term bargain, after which the price has to be raised or the buyer has to look elsewhere. Often the information can be built up piecemeal, with some information from trade magazines and other pieces of information from several sources.

The main principle is that the ideal buying situation is when the you know as much about the supplier's business as the supplier but are spared the risk of actually operating that type of business.

Helping the supplier cut costs

Knowledge of the detail of a supplier's business makes it easier to suggest ways in which a supplier's cost can be reduced, which is one of the main preoccupations for buyers in some large businesses, particularly when dealing with suppliers who are regarded as regular and reliable. The buyer adds methods or design engineering skills to his existing expertise and uses them for the benefit of both parties. Where buyer suggestions reduce costs, the most usual practice is for some but not all of the benefit to be passed to the buyer. In this way a climate is created whereby the supplier wants to talk about the detail of his business because he knows he is likely to benefit.

Whether or not any cost information is obtained, note should be taken of the main cost elements, such as raw materials or components and machining and other processes. The time of people employed to handle or produce the goods and the equipment they use to do so are obviously significant.

Seeing sales representatives when you want to

Sales representatives usually plan their day in advance, sometimes because sales managers want to know where they will be first thing in the morning and first thing in the afternoon so that they can be contacted if necessary. Some firms send their sales people lists of calls, so they have to follow the defined pattern (more or less). If you wish them to call when it suits you, you should follow these procedures:

- Let them know the day(s) of the week and the times you prefer them to call.
- Demonstrate each time that you know what you want.
- Convey the impression that, while you need to see the sales person, there are many demands on your time and you need to be positive. You need conclusive answers and expect to get them,

without the sales person having to refer back to his office or manager. In the exceptional case of the sales representative needing higher authority, ask him to use your telephone to get it.

Sales representatives like to make lots of calls, particularly if they have an incentive scheme related to sales volume. The more calls they make, the more they are likely to sell. A buyer who comes to the point is popular. A buyer who knows what he wants is respected. Selling attracts people who like control of their working day and, particularly, a challenge. Many buyers resent the forceful manner of many sales people and enjoy using their position to deny the sales person a sale. This is a mistake. Any approach by a sales person is an opportunity and should be exploited, either to obtain information (which narrows any gap between sales person's and buyer's expertise) or to obtain a better deal.

There should now be a list of first suppliers and orders can be placed, depending on the picture that has emerged on likely costs and their relationship with funds available.

Buying and selling and the law

This is the point at which the parties are about to enter into a legally binding relationship. Under English law, contract is a large subject on its own but only the major aspects will be mentioned here.

- There has to be an offer and acceptance of that offer. An order is an offer. If the seller signifies acceptance, by sending or telephoning acceptance or simply by delivering the goods, there is a contract binding on the two parties. Unless there is a very obvious mistake on the order, like a misplaced decimal point that inflates the price ten times, the buyer is bound. If, on the other hand, the seller asks for an alteration in the order, that constitutes a rejection and a counter-offer. Only if the buyer accepts the counter-offer is there a contract.
- An offer is held to have lapsed if there is no acceptance after a reasonable period of time. What is reasonable varies with circumstance. An offer to buy perishable food would lapse very much more quickly than an offer to buy a cooker to cook it in.

- Goods must be fit for the purpose for which they are intended. A trader who supplied a decorator with a paint that changed colour a week after application would not have met his obligations, provided the decorator made it clear which colour he wanted.
- A sale that is achieved through a misrepresentation, even innocent, by the seller can be invalid. A drinks machine that is rented by a café owner, on the understanding that it would dispense soup, would be invalid if, when delivered, it only supplied tea and coffee.

Order form design

If, when ordering, the business wishes to use its own order forms, the design should provide for inclusion of

- the firm's name printed in its legal form, so that invoices from the supplier can be accurate;
- any company registration number;
- order number, which can be either printed in advance or entered on the order form as it is prepared; the point of doing this is that it makes it easier to refer to if there are any subsequent problems with delivery or invoicing;
- registered address, if relevant;
- address for delivery, in bold type;
- date;
- quantity;
- product description;
- price;
- confirmation of any agreed discount or rebate arrangement;
- total order value.

If, on the other hand, ordinary letter stationery is used, the same considerations still apply.

Order forms are usually easier to manage systematically, if they are designed to fit in with the general requirements of the firm. These will include

- the need to compare the order details with the goods that are actually delivered;

- checking the order and delivery details against the subsequent invoice;
- progress chasing any late deliveries;
- arranging payment when it is due.

Simplifying documentation systems

Large firms often have complex documentation systems because separate activities, like ordering, progress chasing, checking goods on receipt, checking invoices, are each carried out by different people, often working in different buildings. In a small firm this is usually unnecessary. If one copy of an order is kept and filed in the supplier's file, it can be used for progress chasing (provided a note is made in a diary kept for keeping track of purchases) and for the other checks.

Every time an order is placed, the due date should be recorded. As a daily routine, any goods not delivered on time – or for that matter services not provided on schedule – should be checked with the supplier. Delays should be recorded in the file, so that reviews can easily be carried out with the supplier from time to time. A further advantage of having organized records is that they are particularly useful when contracts, blanket orders or even individual orders are renegotiated. A shortcoming on the part of the supplier can be used to obtain a better deal next time round.

Placing the first order should be the first step on the way to an effective buyer–supplier relationship, with both parties improving their competitiveness as a result. Of course not all supplier contacts will develop in that way, but it is important that most of them do, say those that result in the supply of three-quarters of all goods and services that are required continually. It is a question of a balance between the need for improving the business from time to time and the need to spend more time selling than buying – a natural consequence in an age of surpluses.

For this reason sales people usually have to work harder than buyers to obtain business, so make them work for you! Treat a visit from a sales person as an opportunity, not as a nuisance. If he is inexperienced and seems to be taking up too much of your time, this is a chance to take control of the situation. There are always more benefits to be derived from a commercial relationship, not necessarily lower prices – the salesman will be replaced if he gives away too much – but perhaps more information, or accessories which make equipment easier to use, display material if the business is retailing, or just more information on their range of products.

Applying value analysis

The term value analysis became important to buyers in the early 1960s. It was first developed by engineers, buying for the National Aeronautical and Space Agency in America, who were responsible for spending hundreds of millions of dollars on new products that were designed to perform functions that had never been carried out before. Both the Agency and the supplying contractors were in a new type of industry and the potential for wasting tens of millions of dollars, through sheer inexperience, was considerable. When a product is new it is often more complex in design than later on when opportunities for simplifying it become obvious, through experience of making it – or seeing it made.

The essence of value analysis is not waiting for the passage of time to reveal cost reduction opportunities. It consists simply of looking at each of the parts of a product (in NASA's case it was often a rocket component), or even of a service, and asking the following questions about each of them.

- Is it needed at all?
- If it is needed, can it be made more simply and/or more cheaply?

Out-of-date assumptions

It is interesting how often products start off with assumptions that are later discarded. For example, it was assumed for years that a tyre had to have an inner tube because the heavy main tyre could not possibly be fitted against the wheel rim as it would not be airtight. Had value analysis been employed to question this assumption – and produce the answer that an airtight fit is simply a matter of design – the whole history of the tyre industry might have been different.

In a more informal situation, a car mechanic removed the cover and surrounding parts of the gearbox of his own car for cleaning. After reassembly he was left with various parts – screws, washers and linings – for which there appeared to be no particular use. He put them aside in case they were needed, but the car ran for thousands of miles without apparent disadvantage. Had value analysis been applied, there would have been various advantages:

- Time would have been saved in testing and buying.
- The cost of assembly would have been reduced.
- The car might have been made more attractive to the market, by using the savings to fit an accessory such as a rear seat internal light.

Eventually the manufacturer went out of business, not surprisingly.

The process of value analysis is often assisted by taking the product to pieces and asking the supplier, or someone else with product knowledge, to explain why each is included. Sometimes two or three parts with a similar purpose are included because none of them is considered sufficiently reliable on its own, yet money can be saved, in component cost and assembly, by improving the specification (in the quality sense) of one of the three and discarding the other two.

Production applications

Value analysis can be applied to production processes. A small firm packing fresh produce for customers invited a marketing specialist to visit them. He happened to have a flair for organizing production as well as selling the output, so he analysed the conveyor belt based production process by stages, asking of each stage: 'Is it necessary?'

When he began the exercise, the production line was 150 feet long, with three changes of direction and 20 production line staff. When he finished, it had been reduced to one straight line 60 feet long, with 12 production line staff. Any buyer who could generate this kind of improvement would be in a very strong position when asking for price reductions.

A value analysis specialist was asked to comment on a small chemicals factory and asked why a tank was used at one stage of the production process. He was told that it was used to store partly processed product. He persisted with his question and eventually the production engineer agreed, although he had never thought about it, that the tank was unnecessary and could be removed.

In practice, there has been a tendency for value analysis in large firms to be handled by groups which include buyers, technicians and production people, but not very often a representative of the sales function, so customer attitudes and needs are often forgotten.

Value analysis can be much simpler for the small business. As a buyer you just ask questions, deciding as you look at each part whether you challenge its existence or ask why it is designed in its present form.

Slumbering giants and dwarfs

Having described the various ways of dealing with different parts of the buying activity, there remains an outstanding problem. What to do with an industry that needs work, has reasonable financial stability and products but does not make the responses one might reasonably expect. Sometimes a whole industry, or at least the local part that a particular business needs, responds to buyer enquiries in a very casual manner. Written estimates/quotations are sometimes not given at all or, if they are, without a breakdown of charges between different materials and jobs. Sometimes invoices are not supplied, simply a request for money.

Buyer protection

The best protection for the buyer is to confirm estimates and charges in writing, with copies retained by the buyer. In that way there is a legal basis for goods and services supplied, to which reference can be made if there is a dispute about what was provided or what the charge was. Any legal process will enquire into what was actually agreed, and written evidence, provided it has been previously made available to both parties, will be regarded as providing a more accurate indication of the facts than recollections of what was said or not said.

Although statute and case law, as interpreted by the courts, decide what the law is, the intention in every business transaction is of course to avoid recourse to law, by taking precautions that will discourage the other party from doing so. If anything, a small business needs to be more fussy than a large one because the time required, let alone any costs, is at best inconvenient and at worst disastrous.

Key points

- It helps considerably if buyers demonstrate to potential suppliers that their businesses will be worthwhile customers.
- Methodical analysis of suppliers' potential is important but should not displace instinct and judgement.
- Good buyers show suppliers how to reduce costs and give them some of the benefit.

5

Buying: Completing the deal

Outline

Developing good buying routines includes:

- methodical control of stock
- applying a logical continuity from ordering, through checking receipt of goods to careful invoice checking and controlled payment

Testing new products

Some purchases are for goods that are required infrequently or in small quantities and buying habits can be easily established. In other cases it may be desirable to begin buying a fraction of the total requirement and build up the quantity as experience gives confidence that the right choice has been made. This is particularly relevant in a service business, such as plumbing or decorating, where a new sealant or type of brush may seem much better than what has been used previously. However, there is no substitute for experience and it is better to begin cautiously. Any supplier making genuine efforts to sell its products knows that a customer who buys a new product cautiously is a serious customer and therefore worth cultivating. Products can be rejected for a variety of reasons: unsatisfactory packaging, difficulty in dispensing, poor product quality. If the product disappoints on trial, at least the buyer has had more experience of the industry that supplies him and will be able to buy more knowledgeably as other new products come on to the market. Although it may seem tedious, it is still worth keeping records of why purchases of an unsatisfactory product were discontinued. Memory can be surprisingly short term.

Keeping it simple

As simplicity is particularly important in a small business, there are two factors to bear in mind at this stage:

- The possibility of standardization.
- Ordering regularly used goods on a regular basis.

Standardization means keeping to a minimum the different sizes and different types of broadly similar products. This can mean compromises that are difficult to achieve, particularly in retailing.

There have been experiments, for that is what they turned out to be, in retailing that were based on the assumption that consumers would be interested in receiving the benefits of stock rationalization. The retailer sought to persuade shoppers that his expertise was such that they should accept his choice of a very limited range in return for price benefits. In practice consumers wanted to make up their own minds as to which brands they would buy and resented the withdrawal of what they saw as essential freedom of choice. None of these experiments survived very long.

Retail stocking

However, retailing involves a great many difficult stocking decisions. Some of these are

- which brands/types to stock;
- which sizes to stock.

Few retailers have ideal storage facilities, perhaps because the business has expanded over the years and some store-room space has been converted into selling space. Even brand new premises are not a guarantee of storage space. One new town in England, theoretically designed to provide an ideal balance of residential, industrial and retailing facilities was completed with many shops that had no store rooms. Apartments over the shops were part converted to stock-rooms but this was very far from ideal. The tenants did not relish having to share their homes with boxes of products.

Stocking brands

Although some low-income consumers, particularly pensioners who are less susceptible to advertising because they have seen so much of it, buy smaller sizes as much as brands, brands are for most people the biggest influence on consumer purchasing. The essence of retailing is to attract people into the store and offer a range of merchandise which makes them want to come back. That means brands, especially where the product is so packaged that its particular properties cannot be seen at the point of sale. Some small retailing businesses make extensive use of wholesaler brands. While these usually lack the design sophistication and impact of either nationally distributed manufacturer brands or national chain private label brands, they can still help convey the traditional branding message of consistency and known quality levels to customers.

Therefore a new retailing business will probably do better to use its display and storage space for brands rather than sizes. Experience will indicate which if any of the brands is not worth stocking, so that experiments can be conducted with different sizes. In fact retail development is largely a matter of experiment, once there is a steady throughput of customers. Many businesses have perhaps a few dozen products and any change in that product or service range can have a significant impact on the future of the business. On the other hand, many retailers have hundreds or thousands of products, and introducing or withdrawing one or two can only have a small influence on the business. The risk is very much less.

Eliminating slow movers

A new retailer is therefore watching out for slow movers in the first few months of business. His customers will decide which those are, but he does need a rule of thumb to sort them out. That 'rule of thumb' needs to be developed and varied with experience, but it is based on the fact that in most businesses the majority of sales come from a minority of products. Therefore stock-taking after the first three months should, amongst other things, seek to identify the following.

- The 5 per cent of products/sizes that are the slowest movers. For the purposes of this exercise each size counts separately. If there are 100 different products with, on average, three different sizes each, there would be 300 units in all. The slowest moving 15 units would constitute the 5 per cent.
- The revenue generated by the 15. If it accounts for 1 per cent or less of total revenue, there is an immediate case for considering whether any of the 15 should be discontinued, beginning with the smallest seller. Decisions on whether to discontinue products depend on

  1 whether discontinued products/sizes can be replaced by more profitable alternatives;
  2 profit margins on individual items;
  3 shop and store-room space.

Assessing economic quantities (i.e. the quantity that gives the best unit price, after taking account of storage costs and also interest, if the goods have to be paid for before the retailer is paid by his customers) is different in a small business. The time of the person doing the work is often the time of the owner or the manager. A large business will employ someone to worry about reordering processes. A small business can seldom afford this. In a small business there is always work to do, which means that there is a cost attached to assessing economic quantities. Taking the 1990 London average earnings, as a reasonable personal income for the business person, and adding 50 per cent to that figure for on-costs such as pensions gives an annual figure of £30,000 a year. If the assumption is made that the average small business manager/owner works a 70-hour week, this gives an hourly value to his time of approximately £8.50. If his normal net profit margin is 5 per cent, then he needs to add £170 to his sales to justify an hour's work. In theory it could be argued that such work can be done at a time when no selling is possible but, in practice, preparation for selling, such as arranging mailshots or changing in-store displays, can be done at any time.

Organizing the stock

A general stock control policy is desirable. Stock control means achieving a balance between various conflicting objectives:

- Minimal use of storage space.
- Never losing a sale because of an out-of-stock situation.
- Minimal demands on working capital, which means keeping stock levels low.
- Minimal use of own or staff time in controlling stock.

Stock control always includes counting, in order to find out how much stock you have. The human brain dislikes monotony and counting is very monotonous. Therefore, it is particularly important to arrange stock so that it can be counted easily, quickly and accurately. I have carried out stock checks in many retail businesses where counting stock is difficult because of the disorderly manner in which it is stored. Any under-calculation of stock because not all of it is seen can result in premature or even unnecessary expenditure. It can even result in paid-for stock lying unnoticed for years.

Therefore the following rules should be applied:

- Always keep the same items in the same place. Storing identical goods in two or more different places is the easiest route to stock errors.
- Remember security but never use accommodation for stock that is more expensive than it need be. For example, only frost-sensitive goods need be kept in a heated room. Likewise do not use air-conditioning unless specifically required. Refrigerators or freezers should only be large enough to store goods that need that kind of environment.
- Make the best possible use of floor space, which means using room height to advantage. It is often cheaper to build racking close to the ceiling and spend some money on portable ladders or a kickstep stool which can be moved into position with the foot.
- Use colour labelling as a reminder of where different types of stores are kept and to warn, where necessary, of time limits on products, e.g. use-by dates.
- Use the cheapest storage equipment available. Do not, for

example, buy storage bins if second-hand pigeon-hole shelving will do the job.

- If the age of the product matters, make sure that it is arranged so that the oldest stock is used, or sold, first.
- Arrange goods in a standardized manner. For example, storing tins on shelving to a depth of ten, or radiator valves in pigeon holes in sets of five (of the same size). This makes counting easier.
- Use a form for stock checking that suits your particular business, with products listed on the left, a blank line after each group of five so that the eye can follow each line easily. In the rest of the form, rule columns in sets of three. The first of each set of columns should be headed 'Stock at (date)', the second 'Sale (or use) since last check' and the third 'Ordered at (date)'. Subtracting the current stock from the total of the previous stock check and adding the last order will give the sale (or use) for the middle column. This makes it easier to decide how much is necessary for the next order.
- Frequency of stock checks and ordering varies from business to business. In some businesses, of course, the frequency of the sales person's calls, during which some of them may do the work for you including deciding the order if you let them, is what decides the matter. In others it depends on how much time can be spared for it on any one occasion and how much can be afforded for orders at any one time. Experiment may be necessary in a new business to find out what is most convenient. Often it may be convenient to set a date by which the next stock check should be carried out, especially in outdoor businesses like mobile vehicle maintenance, where the owner often keeps his 'paperwork' for rainy days. Also reordering must take delivery lead times into account.

However expert the owner/manager believes him or herself to be, buying is going to be a learning process. Even if he or she has bought from all these suppliers in the past, those situations can never be repeated exactly. Small suppliers who proved attentive and reliable in the past may have expanded with success and become less personal and more systematic and detached. Other businesses may have been sold to new owners who manage differently. Illness, age, success and failure are frequent influences in buyer/seller relationships.

Using records for future convenience

The start-up phase may have allowed time for full and careful consideration of buying decisions, but it is important to organize ongoing routines so that time is always on the buyer's side. The ability to refer easily and quickly to previous supplier performance is useful when placing fresh orders. Buying in a hurry can be expensive. Knowing what you want well in advance gives you time to get the best deal.

There are other provisions to make for the ongoing routines, to cover buying processes in any firm. So far reference has been made to order processing and progress chasing, both based on a supplier based filing system.

Next comes a procedure for comparing what is ordered with what is supplied. Large firms have what is sometimes described as GRS (standing for goods received sheets, which are order copies used by receiving departments to either confirm that what was ordered has arrived satisfactorily, or define any shortfall in quantity or quality). Some shipments of goods arrive with delivery notes, which aim to define what has been delivered but they have to be checked against what has actually arrived. If no documentation arrives with the goods, they should be checked against the order. Some orders are acknowledged in writing and that acknowledgement may include an alteration – because of an out-of-stock situation for example. Such acknowledgements can be included in the supplier file.

Invoice checking

Finally an invoice will arrive, although some small firms, usually those that are not obliged to by taxation authorities, do without. When the invoice arrives, the first step is to look at it to see if there is any financial incentive to immediate payment. If not it is usually better to put it aside for a few days, so that invoices can be dealt with in batches.

One of the easiest ways of reducing costs is by checking invoices carefully to see if there is an opportunity to reduce it on common-sense grounds. This is not necessarily a reflection on the supplier. Mistakes can be made, despite entirely honest intentions. Those who prepare invoices naturally represent the interests of the seller, which are to maximize revenue, and this can cause the same item to be entered twice but with a different description. In my experience checking for these kinds of errors can widen profit margins significantly.

Next compare the invoice with the order and evidence of delivery, answering the question: 'Can we *trace* evidence that the goods were ordered and delivered?' If the answer is in the affirmative, the next question is: 'Can we *verify* that the invoiced charge is what it should be?' Answering this question is a two-stage process.

1 Is the invoice precisely correct in its terminology and detail? For example, the goods may have been ordered from one company and invoiced by another. Maybe the second company is an associate of the first and has legitimately been assigned the contract but it is wise to check. Payment without complete justification can be very expensive; other errors may have been included. Some additional item that is quite inappropriate, such as an incorrect tax rate or incorrect tax calculation.
2 Leaving aside any errors already discovered, are there any further errors indicated by comparing invoice with order and delivery notes, goods received sheets or simply file notes made at the time of delivery of the goods or supply of the service?
These processes may indicate one or more reasons for delaying payment against the invoice. The remedy is to raise them with the supplier, remembering that this is not just an administrative chore: it is an opportunity to negotiate better terms for what has been supplied. The point was emphasized some years ago by a new invoice verification clerk who recovered more than the cost of employing her by her methodical approach. She listed invoice shortcomings, which had previously gone unnoticed, telephoned suppliers and obtained promises, which were kept, of credit notes.

Payment

After invoice verification comes payment. This too needs planning. If discounts are offered for payment within specified periods of time, these opportunities should be taken, unless they involve overdrawing at a cost higher than the benefit of prompt payment. If there is no specific reason for paying on or by a particular date, then consideration needs to be given to planning payment.

The object of the exercise is usually to have the use of the funds for as long as possible, without reducing the interest of the supplier in continuing to supply. In practice this may not be very long. Payment within two weeks of receiving the invoice is quite common. Suppliers of services sometimes monitor payment timing closely. One small firm offering professional services uses a computer system in its office, which makes it possible to ascertain the promptness or otherwise of payment while the client is still on the telephone.

Each verified invoice in a batch should be marked with a payment date and calculations made to check that the present banking arrangements can accommodate them. If they can, diary notes should be made, in the same diary as the progress chasing reminders, of payment dates. As these dates are reached, cheques can be drawn and mailed.

Care should be taken to ensure that the supplier knows which cheque relates to which charge. This is often most easily done, where the supplier does not provide documentation to accompany payment, by including a compliments slip on which is written the numbers of relevant invoices and credit notes and the amount enclosed.

Consolidating routines

Routines should now be established for the main buying tasks:

- Stock checking
- Ordering
- Receipt or, occasionally, collection of goods
- Payment

These routines should be planned so that they minimize the demands on your time, employing the batching principle where possible, e.g. not checking a single invoice on its own but waiting, unless there are discount or other incentives, until there is a batch of invoices.

Anticipating supplier price increases

Businesses that earn much of their revenue from providing tailor-made goods or services, for which a quotation is made, need to pay particular attention to checking that their quotation takes account of possible differences between anticipated and actual buying prices for anything that is included in the quotation. If there is an increase, a decision has to be made as to how much of the additional cost can be recovered from the market. Alternatively, a decrease in buying costs makes it necessary to decide whether to take the reduction in profit or whether to pass all or some of it on to the customer, in order to achieve a greater sales volume.

The system to allow this kind of check to be made has to include provision for estimating the costs of bought-in materials or components and is most easily done by having a cost figure for each bought-in item. For example, a 'home visit' carpet cleaning business might build into its quotations a specific allowance for cleaning fluid costs for each square metre. This would be based on buying costs so, if these buying costs alter, the cost figure per metre would have to be altered immediately.

Reviews

Reviewing the buying situation should be carried out at regular intervals. The interval should naturally vary according to the following.

- The number of different items purchased frequently.
- The proportion of total costs that are accounted for by bought-in items.
- The rate of inflation. Wholesale price inflation is more relevant to the buying costs of a business but is published in the main media much less often than retail inflation, so the latter is easier to use. The differences between the two are

  1 wholesale price inflation precedes retail inflation because it is measured at an earlier stage of the movement of goods from point of assembly/manufacture to the point of consumption;

2 wholesale price inflation is measured by reference to slightly different goods and services from those of retail inflation.

The review of buying should be based on supplier files, to assess whether each supplier has been satisfactory or unsatisfactory by comparison with each of the standards (price, delivery, ease of ordering, etc.) that were defined when buying began. Less simple and more detailed methods of assessment can be used for each of the buying criteria, but they will inevitably take more time and will not necessarily lead to extra improvements in buying that are worth that extra time.

After the reviews, each supplier should be categorized as follows.

- Entirely satisfactory.
- Not entirely satisfactory but shortcomings are such that they do not justify the time required to take them up specially with the supplier. They can be mentioned next time there is a more routine contact with him.
- Unsatisfactory in some respects but generally a worthwhile supplier. Shortcomings are sufficiently serious for it to be worth taking them up specially with the supplier.
- Unsatisfactory but likely to remain so. Immediate consideration should be given to starting to order from an alternative supplier and eventually, if he proves satisfactory, to eliminating the current one that is causing difficulty.

Even with satisfactory suppliers there may be a case for setting cost reduction objectives. These will differ according to the rate of inflation.

- If the rate is 5 per cent or less, then a reduction in money terms can be realistic, e.g. reducing a price from £1.88 to £1.85 per unit.
- If the rate is more than 5 per cent, then reducing the impact of inflation is the best that is likely to be achieved, e.g. containing an annual increase to 4p a unit (just over 2 per cent) on a product priced at £1.88 a unit.

Working out price reduction objectives takes a little time but makes it much more likely that real benefits will be achieved. Having a figure to go for is very important.

How to go for it is very much the subject of chapter 11, Buying and selling: successful negotiating.

Key points

- Once buying patterns have been established, initial ordering of new products should be cautious, allowing time for determining whether they are sound commercial prospects, before the business relies on them.
- Eliminating slow movers is important, in order to make the best possible use of space and working capital.
- When quoting for customer business that depends in part on supplier prices, always allow for the possibility of increases in those prices, between quoting and receiving the order.
- Review the effectiveness of suppliers at least once a year.

6

Strategic marketing

Outline

Good selling begins with:

- understanding which qualities of a business, as well as its products or services, will appeal to its customers
- constructing a strategy to use those qualities to greatest effect
- appreciating the economics of the individual business, with emphasis on the number of customers required
- a good understanding of the competition

Defining strategy

Strategy may seem to be one of the new management terms that fill some of the newspapers, but even the smallest business, even the start-up in the sitting room at home, needs a strategy. Strategy means deploying resources to achieve a measurable target – which is the essence of business. Resources include the following.

- Time – your time. This is the resource with the greatest potential for profitable, or unprofitable, use. Conscious decisions on allocating time to best advantage are the most frequent decisions to be taken by the owner or manager of a small business. For example, a shop owner may do better to spend time with a buyer rather than a customer, if he has an assistant to serve that customer.
- Expertise – what you have learned before and during your time in the business.
- Money – which you may have provided, or borrowed from a bank, or which has been supplied by other shareholders – or a

combination of two or more. For a few weeks, money can sometimes be provided by creditors but this is very much a short-term expedient.

- Physical assets, e.g. a small workshop on a well-situated industrial estate.
- Intangible assets, such as a customer base, which could come with an established retail outlet bought by a business.
- People, who may include

  1 employees, with an enthusiasm for and commitment to the business (not everyone wants to be a risk taking owner!);
  2 advisers, such as accountants, bank managers or solicitors, with a flair for the particular type of business;
  3 relatives – in some communities small businesses draw their main strength from all-round family support.

Selling with confidence

Successful selling begins with confidence in the products or services that one is selling. Such confidence needs to be based on an accurate appreciation of what is being sold and its merits in comparison with the offerings of competitors. Confidence based simply on boldness or moods of optimism can evaporate if it is misplaced and customers show disbelief too frequently. There is rarely a business that gets an order in response to every sales approach and the ability to handle rejection, at a personal level, is a crucial sales quality. Handling rejection is very much easier if the seller has sound reasons for believing in his products and their usefulness to customers.

An example is the owner of a small hardware store in a suburban shopping precinct who noticed the threat from the large do-it-yourself stores that were being opened within a mile or two of his shop. He was confident of the popularity, with his many local customers, of the range of products he stocked but anxious that he might be vulnerable to large price-cutting neighbours. He visited their stores and was relieved to discover that his prices were competitive. He then made notes of competitive prices for his most popular lines and kept that information by him, in his own shop. Subsequently, whenever his pricing was challenged, which was not very often, he could produce evidence to the contrary. The advantages were

- he had information with which to reinforce his selling;
- that information, whether or not he used it, gave him confidence in the consumer appeal of his products; it made him a better salesman.

Planning a strategy

The quickest route to a sound strategy and sales confidence is by taking an inventory of the business's *strengths*, its *weaknesses*, the *opportunities* open to it and the *threats* that might confront it. To express it in questions:

- In what ways does this business have advantages over its competitors?
- In what ways is it at a *disadvantage* compared with its competitors?
- What could the business do to improve its prospects in the future?
- Are there any possible developments that might threaten its future?

For a small family-run hardware store, answering these four questions might produce the following inventory:

Strengths

- The proprietor has personal knowledge of his products and is not only able to answer questions on what is stocked but also give advice on which products to use in which circumstances.
- Close personal acquaintance with customers.
- The business is within a short walking distance of the homes of hundreds of actual and potential customers.
- Competitive pricing.

Weaknesses

- Limited storage space and consequent need to make frequent visits to wholesalers.

- Limited in-store display space – seriously reducing opportunities for increasing sales through impulse purchases.
- Acute dependence on family for preserving customer goodwill.

Opportunities

- Close acquaintance with customers gives the proprietor and his family the opportunity to ask them which products they would like to buy, that are not presently stocked.
- The lease on the next-door shop expires in three years' time. The proprietor is in his sixties and is unlikely to renew. There may be an opportunity to expand the storage and display space.
- Contact with potential customers can easily be strengthened by distributing leaflets in the immediate area from time to time, with information on products – especially new products – and perhaps special offers. Special offers might include, for example, a free sponge with every 5 litres of paint bought.

Threats

- Competition between local do-it-yourself superstores and DIY suppliers generally may force down prices of staples, like paint, to a point where this small business cannot compete. In consequence, it would have to rely more on sales of slower-moving products.
- Increased road traffic may result in more parking restrictions near the shop.

Constructing a strategy

From this analysis a strategy can be constructed. It might include:

- aiming to increase the frequency of existing customers' visits to the store by featuring six different competitively priced products every week, using window bills and in-store displays;
- increasing the number of regular customers by distributing handbills locally, every three months;
- eliminating the slowest-moving products, especially the larger ones, to allow more room for display and storage;
- joining the local Chamber of Commerce to lobby against increased parking restrictions.

Other applications

For a self-employed trader, such as a plumber, the analysis would be quite different.

Strengths

- Record of quality work in residential property.
- Organized home back-up so that stocks of parts and materials are maintained and well stored; time booked efficiently, invoices despatched promptly and debts collected.
- Above average ability to convert potential customer interest into an order for work.

Weaknesses

- He cannot sell work while he is doing it, except to the customer he is currently working for.
- No cover in the event of illness.
- No promotional literature, relying on personal acquaintances for recommendations for work.
- Most income comes from small, low-value jobs.

Opportunities

- Larger building firms needing experienced plumbers, for work on residential conversions and modernizations.
- Use promotional techniques to attract more business.

Threats

- Market fluctuating with economic cycles, e.g. potential customers postponing work when higher interest rates increase mortgage costs.
- New competitors providing quality work, at competitive prices, and promoting themselves much better.

This analysis could prompt the following strategy:

Strategy

- Install telephone recording equipment so that a response can be made to customer enquiries.
- Approach larger builders and request subcontract work.
- Supply satisfied private customers with reply paid cards for distribution to their neighbours.
- Organize mutual relief availability with another plumber, in the event of illness. This will not deal with the problem of loss of income but it will serve to protect his reputation and enhance his prospects of further work.

A third example is that of a small company, with six employees including the shareholding directors. Its business is the servicing and repair of personal computers.

Strengths

- Expertise in computer fault diagnosis and repair, particularly for one manufacturer's range of models which have a high market share.
- Located in a high population density area with the probability of there being many small computers, in small and medium businesses, which would need their services.
- No local competitors.

Weaknesses

- No sales capability, all orders coming through a single computer and video shop.
- Recent history of complaints of quality of work on some of the less popular models.
- Very limited workshop space, making it difficult to work in a methodical and organized manner.
- The sales agent had to ask customers to bring their computers into his shop, from which point he would have them transported to the repair workshop. Once repaired the transport process had to be reversed, with the customer coming back to the shop to collect his computer.

Opportunities

- Obtain dealership from the manufacturer supplying the models most frequently handled and thus gain access to registered owners of his machines.
- Take over own marketing, once manufacturer support guaranteed – to give better control of customer relations.
- Discontinue handling the computers of manufacturers where problems have been experienced.
- Resolve service and repair handling problems by obtaining larger workshop.
- Possibility that personal computer design would become more 'modular' so that, when a fault had been traced to a particular section of the machine, that section could be replaced easily and the faulty section taken back to the workshop.

Threats

- Manufacturers might find it easier to concentrate resources on new model development, rather than provide reliable customer service support.
- The growth of a personal computer servicing industry might result in the business losing both customers and skilled employees to new competitors.

Strategy

From this analysis might emerge a three-phase strategy. The first phase would include

- Giving the first priority to obtaining a dealership from the main manufacturer.
- Meanwhile searching for better premises but not making a commitment to them until the dealership is secured.

The second phase would entail

- Sending direct mail shots to registered users of that manufacturer's machines, explaining where the business is now located and what it offers.

- Advertising in the local press.
- Sending direct mail shots to businesses in the area.

The third phase would concentrate on offering servicing contracts, with visits by engineers to users' homes/places of work. These can offer a steadier and more predictable flow of work.

The economics of the business

Consideration of strengths, weaknesses, opportunities and threats is made easier if there is a good awareness of the economics of the business. There are five particularly important factors:

1 Transaction size
2 Frequency of sale
3 Number of customers required
4 Gross margin
5 Net margin

Transaction size

A transaction is a sale of one or more products or services at the same time to the same customer. This is critical in retailing for example. A shop can have plenty of customers but have poor profits because the amounts spent at the time of each sale are small. It can be important to encourage the low-spending customer to spend more on each visit.

Likewise a plumber with too many sales based just on changing taps needs to use the customer contact to sell more, for example fitting thermostats to each radiator in a house. The computer servicing business can extend a printer repair to include fitting a larger memory to the computer.

Frequency of sale

Larger transactions are insufficient if customers buy too infrequently. A caterer whose business depends too much on wedding receptions needs new customers too often. Offering to cater for other occasions in the same family, such as special birthdays and wedding anniversaries, which the customer may not have previously regarded as appropriate for outside catering, can be an answer.

Number of customers required

When the average size of transactions and the frequency with which the repeat customers are buying are known, it becomes easier to calculate the number of new customers that are required. This leads to consideration of where those new customers are likely to be and how they can be reached – and how much it will cost to do so.

Gross margin

Many small service businesses have comparatively low overheads and high gross profit margins. That is, they are selling their time and that of their employees. That fact of life can give them opportunities to generate more revenue, for example by offering to provide several services at the same time, at an overall price that is less than if the different services had been priced separately in the normal way.

Net profit margin

On the other hand there are businesses which quote for contracts, for example jobbing engineering workshops quoting for one-off jobs, with too little regard for net profit margins. They quote too often on a gross margin basis and can win a lot of business, but recover too little of their overheads. Preoccupation with sales volume can lead to losses on contracts, which could have been avoided by more thoughtful negotiation.

Competition

Defining competition, in order to work out how to sell against it, is not always as easy as it seems. Competition for a grocery store is not necessarily confined to other grocery stores and supermarkets but can include

- other businesses, such as butchers and greengrocers, adding grocery products to their product range;
- mobile shops, such as milk delivery vehicles, which sell some groceries;
- restaurants offering short standardized menus based on comparatively few ingredients, which price at a level which makes eating out or buying 'to go' (take-away) a real alternative to many consumers.

Similarly secretarial and typing agencies are threatened by the increasing use of cheap word processors, which are much easier for the layman to use in comparison with typewriters. Often their response has been to innovate by introducing such services as foreign language word processing or even an 'English language correction' service.

Printers and print designers are threatened by the ease with which even small firms can acquire page layout software, laser printers and book or leaflet binding equipment.

The right approach to assessing the competition is to ask: 'What sort of people want to buy what I have to offer and from what other sources can they obtain it?'

Personal objectives

The next stage is formulating objectives, e.g. earning enough from a small business to be able to buy a five-bedroomed house in three years. One man set up his own meat wholesaling business. From time to time he took advice from a consultant who specialized in small businesses. He talked to the consultant about the customary objectives in a business, such as turnover and profits. However, the consultant suggested he thought in terms of getting something tangible that he had always wanted but had never been able to afford. The businessman sheepishly confessed that he had always wanted to buy a particular sports car which had a world-wide reputation for its phenomenal acceleration. The consultant promptly calculated the profit target that would provide the car after six months. This target was reached and he bought the car. Within a year he had exhausted his interest in it, partly because its performance was never matched by reliability and he sold it. But he never forgot the lesson and other incentives took its place. Ten years later he was running a business with a turnover of £200 million.

On the other hand, too much enthusiasm in setting demanding objectives can be counter-productive. One of the most common failings in smaller businesses is concentrating too much on sales. The result can be a rapid increase in buying materials for use in the business, or goods for resale, which leads to an equally rapid increase in money required to pay for them before that money can be recovered from customers. This crisis, known as over-trading, can destroy a business if the constraint of limited funds is not recognized. Other constraints can limit objectives, such as limited factory space, or an inadequate supply of potential employees with the skills the business needs. One business employing two highly skilled machinists had to close down because the machinists withdrew their labour when two large orders came in. They could not be replaced and they demanded such large wage increases that the owner felt he was being held to ransom. He took the view that even if the two orders were met there would be other occasions when the experience would be repeated, and he was not prepared to rely on such circumstances for the bulk of his income.

Constraints on success

In the United Kingdom two particular constraints have been identified as being more often related to small business failure than anything else. One of these constraints is tangible – not enough capital – and the other intangible – inadequate marketing. The analysis of weaknesses makes it much easier to identify such constraints at an early stage and do something about them. The computer servicing firm, which experienced difficulties in using a retailer to sell its services, probably avoided a worse fate by recognizing at an early stage that it did not have, at that time, a marketing capability.

Choosing between alternatives

These planning stages make it easier to recognize the main alternatives that confront the business and take decisions between them.

The following are examples of small businesses that have taken this approach.

- The artist who decided to concentrate on painting buildings, rather than landscapes or portraits for example. This brought her a steady flow of commissions from private buyers and also property journals, attracted by her specialist reputation.
- The mobile car mechanic who decided to concentrate on one make of car. This gave him two advantages:

    1. He could work more quickly because of his familiarity with the vehicles. This gave him a higher profit margin on standard charges for regular work such as servicing.
    2. The same familiarity meant that his fault diagnosis was more accurate than his competitors and, consequently, his repair work was more reliable.

- The grocer who, while offering a full range of grocery products, also specialized in cheeses. This brought into the store customers, with a particular interest in cheese, who enjoyed being able to choose from an unusually wide variety and also buy cheese that had been deliberately aged to the point when its flavour was at its best. This specialization gave the grocer a great advantage over his competitors who were selling a limited range in sealed plastic wrappings. While visiting the store to buy cheese, customers naturally tended to buy other groceries as well.

Checking strategic ideas

The strategic wisdom of a new business, which is still just an idea, can be checked out using some of the market research methods described in the next chapter, particularly if it stems from the imagination rather than experience. However, that check can often be made by sounding out opinions from individuals who have no reason to be either in favour of or against the idea.

One new venture was to offer display ideas to small retailers. The would-be independent businessman had worked in advertising and noticed how the large multiples boosted sales by paying attention to customer flow through their stores. Products were arranged to

- make customers walk right through the store – this was achieved by dispersing the staples (bread, sugar, tea, etc.) as much as possible;
- catch the eye by means of vivid separate displays.

He also knew that the large stores looked more attractive because of relatively uncluttered exteriors.

He reasoned that, if he gave the small retailers the benefit of his experience, they would be willing to pay for it. Unfortunately, he went straight into trying to sell the service, without checking it out. He found there were two types of retailers:

1 Those who were keenly aware of the need to present their products in an appealing manner. They saw modernizing the store as a matter for a shopfitting firm.
2 Those with cluttered stores who felt they were struggling to make a living and that they could not afford a service which would not guarantee benefits.

Unfortunately, despite great efforts to sell the idea, the business never became established.

Having taken decisions on the main strategic options, the trader can then proceed to matters of greater detail – the products/services to be sold, their prices and how they should be promoted. Such details are dealt with in later chapters.

Key points

- A successful business often has to choose between major alternatives.
- Success is more likely if the owner has definite personal objectives, which can only be achieved if the business makes it possible.
- There are constraints on rapid results in most businesses, which should not be ignored.

7

Selling: What products and services?

Outline

Decisions on what to sell involve:

- marketing research, with its techniques of sampling, questioning and results analysis
- sales forecasts
- a willingness to introduce new products and ideas and to test them to see if they are right for the business

Marketing research for small businesses

The decision on the main strategy to be adopted should be made after research, which should also be applied more precisely to the more detailed decisions.

The essence of research is collecting information before committing resources. It recognizes that there is a degree of risk (and thus uncertainty) in any business. Research can help to reduce that risk but rarely if ever eliminate it. Research is about the probability that certain events will occur in the future. It means:

- estimating what they are likely to be and thus:
- planning the business in sufficient detail so that the difference between forecast and what actually happens can be recognized easily;
- making corrections to the plan as the lessons of experience become clear.

Many businesses start up simply on the basis of an idea, without research, and then lose more time and more money making major changes.

How marketing research works

The processes of marketing research include:

- deciding what information is required;
- deciding the sources from which or whom the information should be sought;
- deciding what questions should be put to them;
- deciding what proportion of the sources (where there are many of them) should have the questions put to them;
- deciding how the questions should be worded;
- planning the questioning process;
- carrying out the enquiries;
- analysing the answers.

Information sources

Information can be obtained from the following sources.

1 The reference sections of public libraries which can provide the following.

  - Street directories for door-to-door research amongst consumers. Postal code directories can be particularly useful. They often indicate the number of houses in a street.
  - Street maps.
  - Telephone directories, especially those that are separated into trade categories.
  - Trade directories.
  - Chamber of Commerce directories, listing small businesses in a locality, which can be other customers or competitors.
  - Marketing information, which can indicate whether the business you are planning to enter can anticipate growing (or declining) demand.

The excellence of many librarians should be emphasized. They are often willing to help in a general discussion of a research situation.

2 Local authorities can provide

- records of applications for planning permission for the establishment of competitive businesses;
- electoral registers, with lists of adult residents – if research is carried out 'on the doorstep', it will be much more effective if people can be asked for by name.

Deciding what questions should be put is a critical skill. While a visit to a public reference library should not exclude browsing amongst relevant sections to see if any more useful information can be collected, it is important to arrive with a written list of questions, so that the time can be used efficiently.

A potential restaurant owner might want to know

- the streets and number of homes within walking distance (say a quarter of a mile) of the proposed site;
- the location and type of existing restaurants, in or near the probable customer area.

Researching people

Later the restaurateur would need to talk to a sample of potential customers and ask questions about the restaurant visiting habits of those nearby residents.

- How often do they visit restaurants or use take aways?
- Which restaurants do they visit?
- Which do they like and why?
- What do they dislike in a restaurant?
- What are their views on seating and decor?
- In what size groups do they visit restaurants?
- How much do they spend.
- What type of meals do they like to buy?
- What type of drinks do they prefer?
- What are their favourite meals at home?
- Are there any particular meals they would like to buy but cannot obtain in local restaurants at present?

Some of the questions might need the assistance of 'prompts', that is suggested alternative answers, for example main course menus. The advantage of prompts is that they make it easier for those interviewed to provide answers, but they carry the risk that, left to think of the answer on his own, the interviewee might respond with useful information that would not have been included in the prompt.

If time allows, the first questionnaire should be used as a 'pilot', that is the first few interviews should be treated as a test, to see if the questionnaire

- allows the interview to proceed as a friendly conversation, rather than an interrogation which causes people to become inhibited in their answers;
- should be altered to exclude any questions, or include any new questions;
- has the questions arranged in an order that both interviewer and interviewee find easy to follow.

If the questionnaire is inadequate for any of these reasons, it should be altered before any more interviews are conducted. Access to a word processor makes this a job that can be done in minutes rather than hours. Continuing to work with a questionnaire with which the researcher does not feel entirely comfortable can inhibit the whole research process and produce misleading answers.

Careful thought should also be given to the means whereby the interviewer introduces him or herself. There are three general rules.

1 Politeness – conveying the impression that the researcher understands that he is asking a favour, not demanding a right.
2 Coming to the point – the potential interviewee will probably decide in a few seconds whether to co-operate or not. Every word has to count.
3 Carry identification – for example a business card, which can be left with the interviewee. This provides reassurance that the visit is an honest one and not for some illicit purpose, such as obtaining information on whether the house is worth a burglary.

On meeting each prospective interviewee, the interviewer might begin by saying, 'I am researching local interest in restaurants. May I ask you some questions? My name is John Smith.' If this produces the response, 'Why are you researching?' the answer can readily be given: 'I am thinking of opening a restaurant in the area and do not want to go ahead unless there is a demand for it.'

Selecting a sample

Choosing the proportion of people to question in the area would depend on

1 the time available for the research; this in turn might depend on

- the urgency with which the owner would need to generate profits,
- the availability of others, either family or hired help, to carry out the research;

2 the time of day at which it would be conducted;
3 the probable seating capacity of the restaurant – the larger the restaurant the greater the need to obtain reassurance that it would have sufficient customers.

Sampling and other statistical techniques are very important when research is carried out for a large manufacturer distributing nationally a frequently purchased consumer product, such as coffee or cornflakes. They are less important for most small businesses who operate on a smaller scale. Forecasting the sales, for example, of millions of packs of a food product is much more difficult than forecasting the sale of hundreds.

Painless sampling theory

It is useful to have an awareness, if not an understanding, of sampling techniques. The purpose of sampling is to obtain reasonably reliable information on how a large group of individuals or businesses will behave, by obtaining information from a selected part or parts of the total group. There are two reasons for doing this.

1 It saves money.
2 A high degree of accuracy can be obtained from a small sample. A public opinion poll can use a sample of just over 1,000 to obtain predictions, of considerable accuracy, of the voting intentions of tens of millions of people.

There are four sampling techniques which should be mentioned.

1 Random samples, where everyone or everything has an equal chance of being chosen. If such chances are genuine, the technique is considered to give very accurate results, particularly if the total number involved is large. Techniques for actually extracting the sample include using computers, statistical tables of random numbers or the favourite method of raffle promoters – placing ticket counterfoils in a revolving drum, which is stopped every now and then to allow one of the tickets to be removed.
2 Systematic samples, such as every tenth house. This is more relevant to the small business. It avoids the danger of being influenced too much by a group of people who see each other frequently and may have developed attitudes that are completely different from those of the wider group – and are thus unrepresentative.
3 Stratified samples, with random samples from each stratum. For example someone proposing to go into a highly specialized business, like the reconditioning and sale to the public of Welsh dressers (wooden kitchen furniture with cupboards, drawers, a work surface and plate racks) might take the view that research should concentrate on larger houses because smaller ones would not have room for the product. In consequence, the sample might be chosen equally from ten groups of houses, near the proposed site of the business, with seven of the ten being groups of double-fronted houses.
4 Area samples, which might be created for a knitwear business wishing to expand into a national market. Research could be carried out, possibly by telephone, with samples taken from each part of the country; the proportion of each sample to the total number of samples being the same as the proportion of area population to total population. The results would give an indication of the areas from which demand might be strongest and this knowledge could be applied to subsequent marketing.

Research in practice

In practice the largest number of research interviews that are likely to be necessary for a small business is 100, but 40 is often sufficient.

If the questionnaire is well laid out and the subsequent analysis methodical, 40 interviews can provide a wealth of valuable information.

In carrying out the research it is important to look the part, if it involves meeting rather than telephoning or writing to people. Dressing smartly, as if for a formal business meeting, will help to command attention. The research questionnaire should be typed and clipped to a board, rather than simply being withdrawn from a pocket, on the doorstep, and unfolded. Small courtesies matter, like standing back from the door after ringing the bell. If a person is alone in the house, it can be unnerving to open the door and find a stranger two feet away on the doorstep.

A variation in method that is worth considering is leaving questionnaires with householders, promising to collect within a specific time and making sure you do. This can improve the accuracy of answers but it makes it more important to design the questionnaire and covering letter so that they impress and leave no doubt in the respondent's mind as to what is required.

While research is designed to find out what potential customers want, it is important to commission it with an idea of what is going to be special about the business, so this can be checked without making it too obvious in the questionnaire. For example the would-be restaurateur may be a good fish sauce chef and have ideas about making his own fish dishes the main feature on the menu. If his customers are not very interested in fish, the most original fish sauces in the world will not make his restaurant more successful.

The unique selling point

This concept of a business's special feature, that the competition does not have, is known as the USP, which stands for 'unique selling point'. The unique selling point can, for example, be the range of products, or a new type of specialist shop, or a business in an area which had not been serviced previously.

A London plumber used to take his holidays in one of England's most rural counties because he enjoyed the shooting and fishing. He discovered that, in a number of new housing estates, the plumbing was showing early signs of wear. Systems that should have been sound for twenty years were needing attention after two. Plumbers were having to travel from a distance and there were long delays before urgently needed work was carried out. He concluded that there were better opportunities in that part of the country and he moved his business there. Within a year he was working a four-day week, with ample time for his country hobbies. His USP was availability, as is often the case with small businesses.

The most important lesson of this experience is that he checked it out before making the commitment of moving business and home and spending money on advertising his services to people to whom he was a stranger.

The question of availability can apply to time as well as place. Some years ago a number of country grain merchants were taken over by a large multi-national concern. Grain farmers, like most farmers, were accustomed to getting up early and would often telephone their merchants at about seven o'clock. After the take-overs there was no one to answer the phone at that hour, just an answering machine telling them that the office would open at nine. This was a considerable inconvenience because they expected to be well away from a phone by that time. The USP of local availability had disappeared.

Analysing the answers

Analysing the answers obtained from a survey demands a methodical approach. The effort is worth while because the questionnaire forms often contain the means to a successful business. The object of the analysis is to make it possible to achieve an accurate understanding of the total market research process. This is often most easily done by using summary sheets, one for each question, with columns and rows ruled. One row is used for each questionnaire and one column used for each alternative answer. Questionnaires are numbered to simplify the process. The illustration below explains the method, with exhibit 1 showing the results from question 3.

Question 3 How many times in a month do you visit a restaurant?

Questionnaire number	Less than 1	1	2	3	4	5	6	7	8	More than 8
1				×						
2		×								
3					×					
4										×
5			×							
6				×						
7			×							
8	×									
9			×							
10				×						
11					×					
Total	1	1	3	3	2					1

Exhibit 1

The advantages of doing this analytical work are as follows.

- It protects the researcher from the risk of owner/manager generalizations, such as: 'I've always found Dover sole is very popular' (that does not mean it will be, in a new business). Most aspiring restaurateurs have considerable working experience in restaurants and know how to run them. The great unknown in a new site is the attitude and preferences of customers.
- There is a permanent record of the research, in a format that makes it easy to refresh memories and plan follow-up research.

The second opinion

At this stage there are advantages in having a second opinion, either from a business partner or from a friend in another business that is not competitive. If you are working on your own at this review stage, it is all too easy to find evidence that supports your own opinions and ignore evidence that contradicts it.

Examining the competition

Fortified with information about what some potential customers would like, it is time to look at the competition. 'Comparison shopping' in local restaurants is comparatively easy if it is confined to looking at decor, menus and prices. Tasting the product, judging the quality of service and looking out for local press advertising take more time but can give useful information before commitments are made to menus and decor.

Other research uses

Other businesses would use research in a different way. A plumber, for example, might reason that residential work depends on word-of-mouth recommendation, particularly amongst neighbours, and that research should be more dispersed, to, say, two houses in a street but extending the research to a wider area, looking for pockets of dissatisfaction.

A new personnel agency would need reassurance from potential clients that it was worth setting up. An entrepreneur, with substantial management recruitment experience, conducted general research and made a strategic decision to set up such a business in a Canadian city. He flew in from his home in Britain, fortunately without his family who were to wait until the business was on its feet. On arrival he telephoned the firms he had identified on a previous visit as potential clients, met a warm welcome but learned very quickly that he had arrived, as he put it, in 'the eleventh year of a ten year boom'. He returned to his home in England and found employment with one of the established firms without difficulty and with his savings largely intact.

Forecasting sales

Information on what people are likely to buy is vital but it has to be converted into quantities and/or values of product, or services, so that buying and selling can begin. Forecasting is easier if some basic aspects are appreciated.

- The time period of the forecast should be sufficient to cover seasonal cycles, for example a mobile carpet and curtain cleaning business would probably experience peaks in spring and troughs in the autumn. A decision should also be made as to how frequently results should be measured against the forecast, often enough to spot problems before they cost too much but not so frequently that making the comparison costs more, in time if not money, than is saved or earned by the exercise.

- Forecasting is rarely completely accurate, even in the most sophisticated of businesses.
- The main benefit of forecasting is that it gives approximate guidance on what the business needs to do now, in the way of recruiting staff, buying in goods, materials and services, perhaps raising more finance.
- In practice, forecasting is a learning experience. Comparing actual product sales with what was forecast gives practical information on how customers actually behave in a buying situation, which may be different from what they have said they would do.
- Forecasting gives more control. It is easier to try and correct for a shortfall against target, rather than just simply trying harder in the hope that matters will improve. For example, a small grocery business that identified a sales revenue shortfall, and identified it as coming mainly from the confectionery section, could take various steps, such as

  1 moving confectionery to a section of the store where it would be seen by more customers;
  2 giving it more space, if profit margins justified it;
  3 using display material;
  4 buying more price reduction products from the wholesaler.

Safety in numbers

Forecasting in a small business does not require special mathematical skills. Arithmetic is sufficient in most cases. Reasonably accurate forecasting is most easily achieved by applying the principle that the more the forecast is broken down into separate parts, the more accurate the total figure is likely to be. In practice those parts of the forecast that prove to be optimistic are likely to be balanced by those parts that are pessimistic. While forecasting multi-product sales is one matter and forecasting a limited range of services is another, the principle still applies. For example, a grocer could split his sales between

- frozen foods,
- chilled foods – butter, milk, cheese, etc.,
- non-edible products, such as polishes and cleansers,
- fresh foods, such as bread and fruit,
- confectionery,
- canned and bottled foods,
- packaged foods,
- beverages – soft drinks, coffee, tea, etc.

If it was an ongoing grocery business, he would have at least the records of the previous owner, if he was new to the business himself. These would serve as a useful basis for comparison, remembering another standard rule of forecasting – compare forecasts with previous results, if at all possible. Never expect miraculous improvements overnight!

A plumber might segregate sales by

- contracts with builders for renovation of large or multi-dwelling unit properties,
- private house central heating installations,
- major private house plumbing jobs,
- minor repair jobs.

A temporary office staff agency could use segregation by customer size:

- firms employing more than 500,
- firms employing 200 to 499,
- firms employing 100 to 199,
- firms employing 50 to 99,
- firms employing less than 50.

If it is felt that further detail can assist the forecasting process, the forecast can be broken down by time periods, say monthly. This is particularly useful in businesses like plumbing, with the possibility of burst pipe work in winter months.

Creating yardsticks

In forecasting, each type of business has to have its own yardsticks.

The office staff agency might build up its forecast by defining

- the number of likely customer firms in each category;
- the frequency of contracts per firm;
- the average value of contracts, by category.

This reduces the forecast to simple arithmetic.

On the other hand, the independent grocer is unlikely to have time to work out how many he should sell of each of thousands of products and sizes (nor should he, the time is better spent selling). However, he should certainly be estimating sales values for each major product group, e.g. the eight suggested in the 'Safety in numbers' section earlier in this chapter.

A caravan importer needed to estimate sales of his product so that he could supply the manufacturer with estimates. He identified caravan distributors and obtained information on the caravans they had sold in the previous year. He then took into account the prices and value for money he believed his caravans offered and forecast the number to be sold by each distributor, after comparing them with competition. This gave him sales revenues for each and a total for a year.

The research methods described so far have included desk research – for example, looking up information such as electoral registers to forecast shop usage – and interview research on a personal basis by visiting people at home.

Other research techniques

Interview research can also include the following.

- Visiting firms, which usually entails telephoning in advance to ascertain the right person to talk to and making an appointment.
- Telephone research, which has the advantage of saving travelling time and expense but, on the other hand, usually requires a lot of telephoning time, because people are often away from the phone, and is more difficult to carry out because the researcher cannot see the other person and cannot make judgements about his or her willingness to co-operate. There are, however, an increasing number of firms specializing in this type of work and they can

obtain a lot of useful information, for a fee of a few hundred pounds.

There are also several other kinds of research.

Postal research

Postal research involves

- having the questionnaire printed, together with an explanatory covering letter and envelopes for the replies;
- organizing the mailing – and paying for it;
- arranging for a reply-paid service with the postal authorities;
- waiting longer for replies than with personal interview or telephone interview research;
- accepting that only a small percentage will reply and some of those replies will be half completed or indicate misunderstanding of some of the questions (offering a reward for replying, such as a ball-point pen, is a common practice but it adds to costs and administrative time).

Shopping centre research

The researcher asks passers-by to answer questions. This has the advantage of making it possible to carry out quite a lot of interviews in a short period of time, albeit on a very random basis. It normally needs to be conducted by a woman because strangers are much less likely to answer questions from a man.

Discussion group research

This is frequently used by large organizations. However, its purpose and style are relevant.

Its purpose is to collect information on types of goods and services that people want, that they make not think of if confronted with a series of questions in a five or ten minute interview. The format is to invite six to eight people to a private house and a researcher leads the discussion. He will have a check-list of points he would like them to cover. He introduces the topic, starts a tape recorder and lets the discussion flow, apart from prompting from time to time.

This approach could be useful if an entrepreneur was considering opening a shop selling coffee and related products. It would give him information on the satisfactions that some people sought from coffee and help him construct a more meaningful questionnaire, for the main research. It is often the practice to give people who participate in these sessions some kind of a gift, such as a bottle of wine.

The certainty of change

Research and selection of products or services do not end the process of deciding – which products and services? They merely begin it.

The businesses operating in the markets with the more promising futures have to contend with the frequent arrival of new entries, attracted by the opportunities of those markets. At the other end of the scale are markets that are shrinking and attracting few if any new entrants. The fact that a society allows people to establish new businesses means that there is a constant process of change, threatening those already in the market. One large firm estimated that the market for its goods changed by 4 per cent a year. In other words 4 per cent of its business would disappear each year because either products became obsolete or because habitual customers were becoming fewer in number. This meant that £1 in every £25 of sales had to be sought, either from new products or from new customers, every year.

The same challenge applies to small businesses. From a defensive point of view, there are two steps you can take.

1 Conduct market research amongst your customers to see how satisfied they are. Just as a new business may have started up with research aimed at finding out how to beat companies already in the market, so it needs to protect itself against others doing the same.
2 Keep a watch on what competitors are doing. Are they

- introducing new products or services?
- taking current products off the market?

- finding new customers?
- losing old ones?

New product development

New product development is most successful if there is a willingness to take old products off the market at the same time as introducing new ones. In some businesses, such as computer accessory wholesaling, the decisions are often taken by suppliers. Others have to decide for themselves.

Occasionally a low-selling product can be justified because it helps to attract customers. A restaurant may earn a lot of publicity because it offers caviar, even though very few of the customers order it. That is an exception.

An accommodation agent might decide not to take one-bedroom apartments on to its books, after finding they took up too much selling time that could have been used for larger faster-selling units.

A printer might find that he could reduce the range of colours offered and make more money because he could handle more work overall and reduce machine setting-up time.

A retailer could eliminate the slowest-moving lines and give the display space to other products that were already more popular.

That is the negative side.

New product ideas

On the positive side, what are the sources of new product ideas?

- Customers.
- Competitors: following a lead can be second best but it is often better than not following at all – as long as there is no illegality, such as copyright infringement.
- Suppliers.
- Own ideas – sometimes these are completely original, sometimes they are discovered on visits to another part of the country or to another country entirely.

With new products there are two precautions to be taken.

1 Avoid becoming so enthusiastic, before they are proved, that they distract you from selling proven breadwinners.
2 Put them on trial, before accepting them as a permanent feature of the total selling effort.

Test markets

The principle of testing is applied in many business activities. A factory that needs six machines of a new type may well buy one, initially, and only buy the other five if the first one proves satisfactory. An office might change its supplier of computer print ribbons but only buy one or two at first, to see if the quality is satisfactory.

Similarly in marketing, it is often better to start selling a new product on a limited scale and measure the results, to see if it is worth putting more effort into it.

Take a restaurant as an example. The owner wants to add a new dish to the menu but begins by restricting it to one night a week. This gives him an easier opportunity to see if there is sufficient extra profit to compensate for additional food buying and storage requirements – and a more complicated work programme for the chef.

A test market, which can be applied on any scale, is therefore an exercise in measurement of results. Apart from nominating the product or services to be sold, it should define the following factors.

- The time period over which it should be conducted. The less the delay before customers can be expected to come back for more, if they come back at all, the shorter the test needs to be. A new type of tinned fruit product in a grocery store can be test marketed in a month or so, but a new typesetting service, using a rented machine, might need six months of market testing.
- The volume of sales and profit considered to represent success.
- The price – sometimes products need a second test because there are few sales at the price first chosen. A small price reduction has been known to yield a very big increase in sales.
- The method of promotion. It is important to promote, in a test, at

the same level of activity as would be used if the product is adopted permanently. Otherwise results can be deceptive. Highlighting a new menu item can boost sales considerably but that level of sales would not be achieved if it was adopted permanently.

In measuring results, consideration should also be given to noting any significant decline in sales of other products. To take another restaurant example: a suburban restaurant once sought to boost sales on Monday nights, usually the least busy of the week. It offered special meals and cooking demonstrations that occupied the whole of the evening. These were very popular, even though prices were raised to reflect the extra value. Unfortunately, it was noted that sales on the other six days declined by more than they were gaining on Monday. The scheme was abandoned.

Internal competition

Any business is competing for sales with its competitors but, within a multi-product business, the products should be competing with each other for retention in the range. Some large businesses deliberately appoint managers to concentrate on a product or a group of products. Each of these managers tries to sell more and earn bigger profits than his colleagues. The unsuccessful products are withdrawn and other managers appointed to introduce new ones. By reproducing the circumstances of competition within the firm, the firm in itself becomes more competitive with other firms. This principle can be applied in a small business, as long as it is recognized. It is also applied internationally on a very large scale. The Japanese claim that their firms are not all super-efficient, as they are often seen to be in the rest of the world. One reason for the global success of many Japanese firms is that there is often strong competition within Japan itself. This means that the more successful are well equipped to compete internationally.

In South Korea, another fast-growing economy, the banking system will back a business person who invests only a few thousand pounds, by lending millions. This helps start many new and promising businesses. If, however, a business loses money for six successive months, the bank calls in the loan. The business goes into liquidation and the assets are sold to another business person to try and do better. This is another stimulus to internal competition and efficiency but is not yet known, perhaps fortunately, in the West!

Simply switching customer sales from one product to another is counter-productive but, if losses on one product are more than made up by sales of the new product, the addition to the product range is probably worth while. In the end the customers will decide what they want and the business will succeed if it can find out and provide it.

Key points

- Marketing research certainly has a battery of techniques but in its simpler forms it just means asking customers if it is wise to invest in particular products or services.
- Forecasting helps an understanding of how the business actually works, by comparing what happened with what was expected – and finding out why the difference occurred.

8

Selling: Selecting customers

> **Outline**
>
> Running a business, so as to create more customers than it needs, involves:
>
> - understanding that there are many different kinds of customer
> - responding to those differences
> - applying a set of standard ground rules for expanding the business
> - avoiding dependence on price alone
> - managing customer credit so that it enhances the business

A positive attitude

Taking a positive approach to deciding what sort of people your customers are likely to be is better than just waiting to see what happens.

A tailor had a small shop near one of London's main-line stations. He made suits, carried out alterations and repairs for customers and sold accessories such as shirts, cuff links, gloves and ties. To stimulate trade and attract people into the shop, he used to promote these accessory products with window displays from time to time, sometimes with prominently marked price reductions. The success of these promotions depended partly on price but particularly on style, colours and patterns. When asked why his promotions were so often successful, he commented, 'I know my customers!' He went on to explain that this applied in two ways. Either he knew them as individuals and had a good memory for their personal likes and dislikes, or he knew which types of style, colour, etc. were likely to sell well.

Modern selling

Modern selling has changed, from using the same message to all potential customers, to treating them increasingly if not as individuals then as different types of customer. These differences are not just the obvious ones, such as size and place of business but more subtle distinctions in buying attitudes.

An electrical contractor rewiring houses can encounter customers who

- look for the cheapest possible job, or
- want extra power points, of a conventional kind, in all the rooms, or
- are particularly interested in new lighting ideas, such as spotlights in recesses, dimmer switches and outdoor security lights.

He will learn to recognize these different types and treat them accordingly, accepting the economy buyers for what they are and concentrating his main selling efforts on showing the other categories how to spend more.

A car dealer will recognize and record those customers who like to replace their existing model as soon as it is made out of date by model changes. The dealer will send them details of such updating by post, when they occur, and remind them that he can accept their current model in part exchange.

The wine shop manager finds out from some of his customers the meals they most enjoy at home and then displays the wines to match them, suggesting that the customers enjoy the two together. The shop fascia and a clean and orderly interior may attract customers inside but positive suggestions for buying will create sales.

Importance of not selling on price alone

All these selling efforts are obviously directed towards obtaining more customers, but the critical point is that the more customers a business has the less dependent it is on selling on price alone. A business that sells on price alone is making a public statement that it has nothing else of particular merit. Ideally, a business should have more customers than it needs; the wine shop that can afford to ignore demand for a cheaper wine because it can use the display space effectively for a higher quality higher margin wine is in this fortunate position.

The restaurant that is full or nearly full for lunch and dinner every day of the week is also in this fortunate position. In one case a restaurant had a small high-cost site in one of the most fashionable areas of a large city. Seating capacity was severely limited and confined to one small room. There could have been difficulties in generating enough revenue to cover overheads and other costs but, the owner adopted a strategy to deal with this problem. He offered attractive menus and deliberately spartan accommodation. Instead of having tables with chairs round them in the middle of the room, he lined the walls with wooden benches, with rectangular wooden tables without tablecloths and wooden chairs facing the benches on the other side of those tables. Thus the restaurant consisted of two rows of tables with movement of customers and waiters in the space in the middle. Customers were seated very close to each other, even if they were strangers. Far from putting customers off with the lack of privacy, the restaurant became a popular social centre, attracting people who were uninhibited by the congestion and hearing strangers' conversation as easily as they could hear what their friends were saying. The first impression on entering was the hubbub of conversation. What the owner had done, wittingly or unwittingly, was to segment his potential market.

Another restaurant with more spacious premises might decide to concentrate on the one-sitting dinner business. This would mean organizing the facilities to give customers value for money, so that they would happily stay in the restaurant for three hours. Such facilities might include: a separate lounge for pre-dinner drinks and ordering the meal; an elaborate design for each course so that it almost became a meal in itself (one restaurant kept its customers happily occupied on the first course for an hour or more, with toast and a whole range of pâtés); comfortable seating and spacious tables; waiters always offering a different wine with each course and making positive suggestions, rather than just presenting large wine lists; at least four or five courses; encouraging guests to linger over coffee and liqueurs.

The main theme is subtle and unobtrusive selling throughout the meal, not just at the beginning. This style of restaurant does, of course, depend on the availability of a sufficient number of customers, with the means to pay the high prices that must be charged, for the operation to be economic.

Segmentation of customers

Segmentation is increasingly used in selling to differentiate between different types of customer and thus sell to each in a more effective way. For example, the restaurant might have segmented its customers further into evening diners who wanted a good night out and the 'lunch trade' who only had an hour or so to spare and preferred a simple menu with mainly non-alcoholic drinks.

On a simpler level, a professional firm criticized one of their number because he had the 'wrong kind of clients', which were defined as clients who did not pay their bills! Had their business been sought on a more gradual basis, which would have allowed the firm to monitor the promptness with which they paid the first small bills, the risk of loss would have been reduced.

Identifying the different kinds of customer means asking questions that are right for the individual business. Some are obvious, others more subtle. These questions can relate to several factors.

1 Apparent spending power.
2 How close to or distant from the business they are. An extreme example is the motorist in Hertfordshire who took her car to a Manchester garage for servicing because she felt it was the only one she could trust.
3 Age.
4 Sex.
5 Occupation. An area with many working wives could mean that a mobile shop operator might do better to work in the evenings.
6 Size of household unit. This has a critical impact on, for example, a shoe retailing and repair business.
7 Motives for buying. These can be harder to discover but can include the following.

- Social pressures, buying because a neighbour or friend has one. These motives are recognized by building specialists, who deliberately try and sell a loft extension or conservatory in a new area because they know some neighbours will want one as well.

- A tendency to exhibitionism, buying a product because it shows an individual to be different from others. An example is buying extra headlights, which are not really necessary, for a car.
- An enthusiasm for new products because of the pleasure of having the new experience of owning them.
- Family conformists, who buy a product or obtain a service from a particular firm because the older generation did so.
- Business conformists, who buy for their businesses as they have always done because it is easier that way and they get paid just as much.
- Fear, which can prompt buying, for example, of burglar and smoke alarms, or the replacement of armchairs with new ones because they have been made with a more fire resistant foam.
- Buying not just the product but advice as well. A good seller will recognize when a customer is uncertain, not because he or she does not want to buy but because, while he or she understands the need, the product required is not known. Some of the most successful small pharmacy businesses have become successful by recognizing this. A sympathetic reception and suggesting the right remedy (where a visit to a doctor is unnecessary) have served to build prosperous businesses.
  The value of advice is often underestimated, especially by those who seek it. A self-employed auto-electrician (who specializes in correcting defects in the electrical circuits of cars) has a notice in his workshop: 'Advice will be charged for.'

Ground rules for business expansion

In business, change is part of the natural order. No business can be realistic and operate on a policy of 'stand still'. The intention to expand, if only to make the business more resistant to competition, is very important, even if it is only intended to expand profits by changing the products or services offered.

Some approaches to business expansion have already been

described but knowing how to plan it is easier if the following four methods are remembered:

1 The method, which carries the least risk is to sell more of the existing range of products or services, to existing customers.
2 Selling new products to those existing customers.
3 Selling existing products to new customers.
4 Selling new products to new customers.

The last is the most difficult but generally speaking finding and keeping new customers is more difficult than finding new products.

Pricing

Pricing mistakes

Pricing is close to products and customers in importance. The most frequent pricing mistakes are the following.

- Deliberately under-pricing all known competition. The whole point of selling is to demonstrate that the product or service differs from competition in as many ways as possible. A claim to cheapness is an implied claim that it cannot compete in any other way. It also risks the buyer taking the attitude that, if the product sells only on cheapness, why not make it even cheaper.
- Making confident but essentially vague claims about quality and then pricing well above the market.
- Pricing on a cost-plus basis without regard to competition. Many businesses have made this mistake, which can produce two particularly inconvenient results:

  1 The business is lost because the same value can be obtained elsewhere, at less cost.
  2 Competition is undercut by such a substantial margin that the customer worries about getting good value. Even if the supplier gets the business, he may not know and go on losing profit opportunities.

- Applying a single yardstick to pricing such as a standard percentage mark-up. One firm marked up all its products by 10 per cent, even when it obtained temporary price reductions from its suppliers. This meant that it passed on the reductions *and more* even though there was no indication from its customers that they were dissatisfied with the usual prices. For example, if it bought a product at £1.00 in normal circumstances, it marked it up by 10 per cent to £1.10, thus yielding a 10p profit. If it bought for 90p it marked up to 99p, taking a profit of 9p. Alternatively, marking up a wide range of products by the same percentage margin ignores the fact that customers may have perceptions of value that allow prices and margins to be varied considerably from product to product.

Influences on pricing

Pricing is more important in some situations than others. It depends on various factors.

- The frequency with which the product or service is purchased. Breakfast cereal pricing means more to the consumer than light bulb pricing.
- The importance of reliability or safety in the product. If the customer has confidence in the product, an extra 10 per cent on the price may well be sustainable.
- The ease with which a cheaper alternative can be acquired. Holiday hotels reduce their rates in winter because demand is much less and customers can be more choosy.
- The knowledge the customer has of the particular product, what it offers and where it can be obtained. Different customers have different interests and product knowledge varies widely from one to another.
- The total cost to the customer of the product. The more it costs the more it is worth the customer investigating it. For example, one individual spent six months looking for his next car, first collecting information on the alternatives then, having decided which car he wanted, looking for the best combination of price and service. He eventually bought from a broker 150 miles from home (at an 18 per cent discount) and arranged local servicing.

Perception of value

The right price for a product or service depends on a customer's perception of value. That value is affected by a range of influences

- The extent to which the product appears to provide the main benefit for which it is being bought, for example, a radio with demonstrably clear reception.
- The special features of the product: major features (like the number of wavebands on a radio) and minor features (like colour coding for waveband indicators).
- The general presentation of the product – style, colour etc. For example, a cleaning/home help service has smartly painted vans and issues overalls to its cleaning staff.
- The reputation that comes with the product because of its manufacturer and perhaps because of the place where it can be bought. Two identical toys were on sale in department stores within three hundred yards of each other. One store had a local reputation and priced at £1.15. The other store had an international reputation and priced at £1.75!

Pricing does not stand alone but forms part of the selling effort. Sales methods and sales promotion are the subject of the next chapter where they are dealt with in detail but in the meantime attention must be given to the question of getting paid.

Credit control

If the business is selling goods or services on condition that payment is made before delivery or supply of the service is complete, then the problems are more likely to be those of security until cash and cheques, where used, are banked.

If credit is offered it should be as a deliberate policy to attract customers and take account of the actual cash demands on the business. For example, some electrical and building contractors, commissioned to carry out comparatively minor tasks such as rewiring a home or repairing a roof, will ask for payment for the materials to be used, when the job starts, and invoice the remaining charges a fortnight after completion. Another variant, used by businesses selling repeatedly to the same customers, for example petrol stations, is to take a deposit before the first sale and invoice the customer at regular intervals. This prevents forecourt attendants or cashiers from having to do more than obtain a signature at the time of each sale.

The cost of credit is significant and should not be forgotten. This takes two forms:

1 Operating the credit system, which means employee's time and the cost of correspondence, telephoning and other forms of communication.
2 Paying the bank for an overdraft facility or, alternatively, missing the chance to put the money on deposit and earn interest.

A more serious complication can arise if an overdraft is required (or an additional overdraft) and the bank refuses to provide one. This leaves the borrower with the awkward task of either keeping his creditors at bay a little longer or finding another bank, which is very time consuming.

If credit is offered, it is important to have a good reason for it, calculating how much extra business it will bring, over a specific period of time, and how that extra business will affect the profitability of the firm. Having made those estimates, it is important to keep a record of them, so they can be compared with what actually happens and lessons can be learned from the experience. If on the other hand credit offered may be simply following the custom of the trade, then there may be a case for experiments with either shorter or longer credit, to see if they are commercially beneficial.

Credit limits

In operating a credit control system, the supplier must consider the following.

- The maximum amount of credit to be offered to each customer, i.e. his credit rating. In practice a series of credit limits appropriate to the type of business should be operated. For example they might be £100, £200 and £300, so that the decision as to how much credit is offered is considerably simplifed. In theory a small business can obtain information on the ability of some of its

customers to pay their bills, but this may not be practical. Small businesses often make most of their sales to small customers. Even if information were to become available on them, it would become out of date very quickly. A householder can lose his job, or spend his cash reserves on a new car. A business can suffer a sudden loss of sales. The best solution is to offer credit with great caution, however attractive the sales prospect is. Start at the bottom limit and let the customer build up a creditworthy reputation. Even then caution is advisable. Customers are much more accustomed to credit than they used to be and are much less frightened by it. It can happen that a customer deliberately builds up a good credit reputation and then fails to meet a large debt.
- For how long the credit will be offered and whether any discount percentage for on time payment should be offered.

Debt collection

Collecting debts can be a harsh experience for the small business. All too often it causes anxiety or a feeling that it is casting doubt on a business person's ability to provide the service or goods for which he or she seeks payment. There are various reasons for delayed payment of debts:

- Goods have not in fact been delivered.
- The customer has been invoiced in error and is waiting for the supplier to find out and acknowledge it.
- The customer does not believe he has received value for money.
- The customer has forgotten the debt.
- The customer cannot/does not want to pay at the moment.

Collection system

The debt collection system to be used should include an invoice designed to show clearly

- the legally registered name of the business, if there is one; failing that the name by which the supplier is usually known;
- its address, telephone number and fax or telex numbers if relevant;
- the formal name of the customer, together with his address;

- The date;
- the date payment is anticipated, or notification that payment is due immediately;
- an invoice reference number;
- details of amount owing and why;
- any tax to be added in;
- total due;
- VAT number.

Timings are suggested for the remaining stages of the procedure and can of course be varied to suit individual circumstances.

If payment is not received within two weeks of the due date, a statement should be sent. This is similar to the invoice to which it refers, except that there is no need to give justification for the charge(s).

Thereafter, the following letters should be sent at fortnightly intervals, until and unless payment is received:

- A polite reminder that the debt is outstanding and should be paid immediately. (A telephone call at the same time is often effective.)
- A firmer and more abrupt request for the money.
- Another reminder, together with the statement that unless payment is received within a fortnight, consideration will be given to taking legal proceedings.
- A statement that the matter has been referred to solicitors, that legal proceedings may be instituted and that the courts frequently give judgement that debtors should meet at least some of the creditor's interest and legal expenses.

Legal action should be a last resort. It costs money, often takes a long time and, even worse, can take up time that would be used for earning money. A self-employed electrician could lose half a day's work going to court and this cost can make debt recovery prohibitive.

One variant on this debt collection process can be considered provided the timetable is not interrupted – a visit to the debtor. There is considerable wisdom in the old saying: 'The best way to collect a debt is to go and get it.' Whether you do depends on

- whether you wish to continue the business relationship;
- whether you can afford the time.

The advantage of the step-by-step system is that it enables the process of debt collection to proceed, with a minimum of strain on the creditor. However, three developments may interrupt it:

1 Part payment may be received, in which case the process of debt collection should be sustained, for the remaining debt.
2 The debtor may dispute the obligation, in which case a negotiating situation applies (negotiating is explained in chapter 11).
3 Information is received that the debtor's business may be about to go into liquidation, in which case another old rule applies: 'The best time to collect a debt is now.'

Key points

- Know the most common pricing mistakes and avoid them.
- Accept that it is how customers see the business that counts.
- Reduce anxiety about debtors by operating a standardized debt collection system.

9

Selling: Skills, methods and management

Outline

This chapter is concerned with:

- sales techniques
- taking initiatives to contact customers
- deploying sales staff
- special approaches for selling to large companies
- helping customers sell

Concentrating on the customer

Selling skill is essential in anyone who is in charge of a small business, but the thought need not cause anxiety. It is not necessary to be an actor or a flamboyant personality. The best sales people have become good at it by being themselves and focusing their attention on the customer, not worrying about the impression they are creating. Good sales people often comment that they have learned not to worry about what people think of them. If one customer rejects them, they quickly move on to the next one.

In a sense the best sales people are good because they have learned to handle themselves in the face of rejection. Good selling can mean keeping going after six buyers in succession have told the sales person to go away. One salesman rose to be sales director of a large company within eight years, responsible for nearly 400 salesmen and sales managers. He had no experience of selling when he joined. He received initial training and set out to make his first call on a customer alone. This customer took exception to him on sight, picked up a chair and used it to force him out into the street! He just went on to the next customer.

Asking questions

The days have gone when a sales representative assumed he knew exactly what his customers wanted and started a sales call by talking confidently about his product. Selling is much more successful if the sales person begins by asking questions and uses the information those questions produce to suggest how the customer might buy. The essence is asking questions that generate answers that allow the seller to make a specific suggestion. There is no advantage in a shoe retailer, for example, asking what colour trainers a customer wants if the answer is a colour which is out of stock. On the other hand an accommodation agency, with two- and three-bedroomed but not four-bedroom apartments on its books, should ask clients coming into a branch: 'Are you looking for a two- or three-bedroomed apartment?' rather than: 'Exactly what are you looking for?' If the prospective client replies that he is looking for a four-bedroomed apartment, the sales person has an uphill task on his or her hands. It may be that the client was not at all sure what he wanted but thought of a number when he was pressed for an answer.

Retail applications

This key principle of asking questions has particular applications in retailing, when it can be used to suggest additional purchases:

- The sales person in a shoe shop, who follows up a shoe sale by asking whether the customer needs any shoe laces or shoe polish, for example. Perhaps that customer does, but had forgotten about it.
- The hardware shop owner who sells paint and then asks whether the customer needs a roller or paint tray. The customer may have them already but they may be paint encrusted and difficult to use. As a result the customer leaves the shop after buying more than he intended but still well satisfied.
- The jobbing printer, who receives an order for replacement stationery in the early autumn and takes the opportunity to ask the customer if he would like to order personalized Christmas cards.

Overcoming objections

Asking questions is a technique that is particularly important in dealing with objections, another vital sales skill. The best sales staff do not necessarily avoid objections by 'fast talking'. They use the objections to earn the customer's confidence. Overcoming objections is very much easier if it is recognized that the stated objection may not be the real one. A child may say a pair of new shoes are uncomfortable because she knows that objection will count most with her mother, when the real reason is that she does not like the colour. The sales person may have good reason for believing that there is nothing wrong with the fit. The solution to that selling problem is to suggest she tries on another pair of a different colour and not to waste time on asking questions about comfort.

A home visit carpet and upholstery cleaning firm may take an order for carpet cleaning and go on to suggest that some of the armchairs in the house could conveniently be cleaned at the same time, only to meet an insistence that it was unnecessary because they are clean enough anyway. The sales person knows this to be untrue, but would probably be wasting his time if he argued about it. There is probably another reason. Perhaps the housewife is worried about the total cost, needs to think about it but does not like to say so. In which case the correct question may be, 'May I leave it until we have finished the other cleaning?' This takes the pressure off the customer without abandoning the prospect of an additional sale.

The worst sales staff

Probably the worst sales staff are those who make a definite sales proposition to a customer, encounter reluctance to buy and deliver lectures along the lines of: 'I cannot spend too much time here,' or 'In your own interest you have got to make up your mind.' Believe it or not, there are people like that, who confuse being positive, which is a sales virtue, with being aggressive, which is a definite liability!

Judging personalities

On the other hand, it is true that different customers react to different sales people in different ways. It depends on the way personalities react to each other. The same sales person can encounter customers who

- seem relieved to receive positive suggestions, or
- resent any suggestions and take the attitude: 'Tell me what you have and I will tell you what I like', or
- are receptive to any suggestions, provided they are rationalized.

The sales person needs to recognize and adapt to these very different attitudes.

Closing the sale

An important part of a sales person's armoury is knowing how to close a sale – getting the customer's commitment to buy. This is the point when the customer seems to have decided, or nearly decided, to buy. There are two particular rules to remember:

1 Ask for the order. Many sales people present their case very well and talk constructively with the customer, but hesitate to ask for the order because they feel that it is the 'make or break' point and they fear rejection. In practice most sales situations are retrievable. In a sense selling is the ability to come up with the answer to problems, whatever the objections.
2 Close the sale at the first possible opportunity. Many a sales person has lost a sale because he could not believe his luck when he met a customer who said immediately that he wanted to buy. Despite this most positive of 'buying signals' such sales people insist on going through the presentation they have prepared. This prompts the customer to think of objections and he changes his mind.

There are various types of close:

- The alternative close, when two alternatives are suggested: 'Would you like three or four?'

- The concession close: the sales person deliberately suggests a slightly larger order than he thinks the customer is prepared to settle for. The customer responds by demonstrating his independence by nominating a smaller quantity and the sales person accepts promptly.
- The command close: 'I'll write out the order and you can sign here.'
- The silent close: the sales person deliberately stops talking and waits. In the silence that follows, the customer feels he ought to say something and so he orders.

Practising selling

These comments on selling prompt the question: 'How do I acquire these skills?' The answer is, by practice. The greater the sales experience the more the sales person is likely to use these skills in his own way, so that his approach to people is natural and comes across as genuine. In the early stages, it helps to remember that

- persistence is all important, not in persisting too long in the face of an individual refusal but in moving on to the next opportunity;
- it is unusual for a customer to be lost forever; often re-encounters can be productive, provided some new and interesting information is given to the customer;
- learning from successes and failures is vital.

Second opinions

For the one-man or one-woman business the problem can be a lack of a second opinion, particularly after a bad day when there have been few or no sales and nothing seems to have gone right. There are two ways of dealing with this problem:

1 Sharing problems and discussing solutions with friends and acquaintances in non-competitive businesses.
2 Using the services of a sales training consultant, on an intermittent basis, for example half a day a month. The consultant joins in a review of the previous month's selling and agrees a

general sales plan for the next month. Such consultants are best hired on the basis of a recommendation from a trusted source, or from an organization that maintains a register of consultants of proven quality. No contract should be made with them until they have visited you and agreed terms of reference and fees.

A consultant is essentially an adviser and different from an agent, who may do some selling in return for a commission. In some circumstances, using acquaintances as sales agents has worked very well but there can be difficulties. If the agent is not working full time for the business, it is difficult to know when he is going to bring in business. Sometimes, he may make bold claims for the business that cannot be demonstrated in practice. The problems are those of contact and control.

Making effective contact

In all but the lucky few businesses, initiatives have to be taken to contact customers and encourage them to buy. There is a scale of contact effectiveness, with the most effective form of contact being the most expensive.

- Meeting people to sell to them is that first form of contact.
- The telephone comes next, cheaper than face-to-face but presenting the telephoner with greater difficulties in attempting to control the customer.
- The personalized letter, which can be sent by facsimile transmission (fax) in many situations. The postal service is of course much cheaper but can result in the letter being ignored because so many selling communications are being received. A part solution, used by some small businesses, is to have the envelope addressed in handwriting, which prompts much more curiosity about the contents.
- The printed circular, the cheapest but probably the least effective form of communication. Design can be used to make the letter and envelope more eye-catching but this is a widely used practice already.

These are the tools of the selling effort and their use needs to be organized to suit the individual business. With a one- or two-person business it depends to a great extent on the people who are going to do the work. Some people enjoy person-to-person contact, either face-to-face or on the telephone, but have a strong disinclination to engage in the writing and administration that the cheaper methods call for. However, even they have to keep records so that the effectiveness of their selling efforts can be measured. Such records should show:

- who was contacted and their whereabouts (if known) for recontact;
- total number of contacts;
- number of orders resulting;
- delay between first contact and first sale.

This enables an informed decision to be made about

- follow-up efforts;
- further use of the particular kind of sales contact.

Before any kind of selling effort is organized, there needs to be a clear view of the objectives of the exercise. Is it to

- obtain orders straight away, or
- encourage customers to ask for an estimate, or
- encourage customers to visit the seller's premises where he or she can be persuaded to buy.

Writing sales letters

For those whose inclinations do extend to writing sales messages, or whose businesses are large enough to allow the employment of others to do the writing, certain guidelines should be followed:

1 The message should begin with an eye-catching incentive to read on. This incentive must relate to customers' interests not necessarily those of the seller. For example, 'We are the best carpet cleaners' does not necessarily impress because it begs other questions such as; 'By what standards?', or 'Who says so?' A headline such as; 'The carpets we clean last two years longer' is much more meaningful because it offers a promise of benefit that can be evaluated by the customer, who knows how much she paid

for the carpet. At the same time it does not always pay to make a promise that is too specific.

2 The next part of the letter or circular should state clearly why it has been sent. For example, 'We would like to give you an estimate of the cost of cleaning your stair carpet' – provided such a letter is only sent to people living in two or more storey houses!

3 There should be substantial and convincing reasons as to why the customer should respond to the invitation. These might include

- ten years experience;
- *X* satisfied customers in certain specified areas, with an offer to show the customer genuine testimonials;
- each contract supervised by a foreman/manager/the owner;
- follow-up telephone call, three days later, to check satisfaction.

4 Finally, what is known as the 'clincher' – the end of the letter which is intended to prompt a positive response. This might be an invitation to ring the seller at any time or, more expensively but even more positively, a statement that the seller will telephone within a certain time. This is intended to demonstrate that the seller is seriously interested in doing business with that particular customer.

Effective sales use of the telephone

Whatever the previous circumstances, any telephone call made with the intention of selling or opening the way to a sale should be scripted. As with telephone research, a script is a short written statement of what should be said at the beginning of the call. It should be drafted with a good understanding of the customer's position. If called at home, he or she may be fearful of a possibly hostile intrusion into his or her privacy. Householders have been made cynical by experience of ill-trained and inexperienced telephoners trying to sell them something. If at work, he or she may resent another demand on his or her time. Apart from the script, there are several other sales points to remember.

- Avoiding inaccurate statements like claiming you are carrying out research, when in fact your intention is to sell. The phrase 'We are carrying out a survey' has been so often abused that it should not be used unless it is an honest statement of fact.

- Maintaining courtesy during the call.
- Adopting a businesslike posture. This sounds quaint but it is important because, for example, a slumped posture in a chair can result in over-casual and even indistinct speech. Certainly, the telephoner should sit upright at a desk or table, with his script, information and notepad in front of him. Some of the best telephoners stand up for important calls because they feel it gives their telephone manner a crisp and urgent atmosphere!
- Giving your name and if possible the name of your firm at the beginning of the call. Anonymity can seem evasive or even sinister.
- Avoiding the trap of saying, for example: 'I expect you remember our letter.' This exposes the telephone seller to the simple rebuff – 'No'. He is now at a serious disadvantage. If, on the other hand, he explains himself in a straightforward way and the other person recalls receiving the letter, he can simply say he is glad he received it and go on to his proposition.

The following is a good opening statement to a telephone call:

> Good evening. My name is Smith of Cleanwell Limited. I am calling to ask if you would like to use our carpet cleaning service next week. We have a number of visits to make near you and would be able to include you if that would suit you.

It is inevitable that some or even most of such calls will meet rejection. With experience, answers to some of the objections can be added to the script and used if necessary. The extended script might include:

> *Objection*: 'We had them cleaned last year.'
> *Answer*: 'How often do you have them cleaned?' which can open the way to regular contact.

or

> *Answer*: 'We also have an upholstery cleaning service. Can we help you there?'

Selling not offering

In selling it is important to do just that, which means making a definite proposition. Just telling people about all the products or services you have available is not selling, it is offering. The difference is that, in nominating a specific, the seller is moving as quickly as possible towards a proposition that may result in 'closing' a sale. Suggesting a wide range of alternatives is handing the initiative to the buyer, who may reject them all (if only because he is too busy to think them all through), which puts the seller in a position which is difficult to retrieve. If, on the other hand, there is a definite proposition which is rejected, the seller can more easily move on to the next one.

Deploying sales staff

If the firm is large enough to employ one or more full-time sales people, this generates a need for planning and control so as to obtain the maximum economic benefits from the selling effort. To do this, various items of information are required.

1 The area to be covered.
2 The number of calls a sales person can make in a day. This depends on

- the number of products he has to sell – the more he needs to talk about, the longer the call will take;
- the complexity of the products or services;
- the distance between the customers;
- the ease of travelling between them – they may be close together but urban traffic congestion or a shortage of parking can reduce the number of potential sales calls.

3 The potential volume of business each customer is likely to provide. This can vary considerably so that some need a more frequent call than others. As regular sales patterns develop with customers, so they can be classified according to size. For example, if average sales per customer per month vary between 5 and 55 units, they might be classified as

- large, if they buy between 41 and 60;
- medium, if they buy between 21 and 40;
- small for 20 or less.

The advantage of such a classification system is that it makes control easier. Decisions can be made, for example, to increase call frequency on large accounts and decrease them on small accounts.

Targeting and training

Other tasks for those managing a sales force, however small, include the following.

- Setting targets for individual sales people, quantifying target sales of each product or group of products, within suitable time periods. Setting targets is a device to let sales people know what they have to do to contribute to the total effort of the firm. It needs to specify how much should be sold of each product/service, in each relevant time period. Banks often ask businesses for monthly cash flow forecasts, so forecasting a month at a time is often sensible.
- Training them to plan effective use of time. This basically means aiming to complete a minimum number of sales calls in a day.
- Training them to plan each sales call effectively.

An example of the last item is the case of a young sales manager who took over a team of salesmen and began by spending a day with each of them, visiting customers. At the first call the first salesman parked outside and started to get out of the car. His manager stopped him:

'Before we go in, let me ask you: why are you going to see him?'

The salesman replied: 'To sell him!'

'Right,' said the manager, 'Let us ask ourselves how much he can reasonably be expected to buy and why he should buy from us anyway.'

The same technique was applied to each salesman in the first few weeks. After that they went into each call with a clear set of objectives and the ability to justify the propositions. They had a plan, based on their previous knowledge of the business, but were of course prepared to vary it in the face of objections. By no means all of their propositions were accepted but within six months the total sales of the team had increased by three times!

Controlling the sales effort

An easy-to-use sales control system is necessary. This should include:

- a record for each customer, with planned and actual sales of each product for each call;
- a daily sales report with a record of each call, sales achieved in it and any expenses incurred.

Such records should not only enable the employer to supervise the sales person, but help the sales person to become more conscious of his own performance and where it could have been improved.

Effective incentives

As a general principle, the less management advice and help a sales person receives, the greater the proportion of his earnings that should be tied to results. Incentives can take many forms.

- Bonuses related to company, sales team or individual performance, against targets.
- Commission on sales. This can be a percentage, increasing with the total volume of sales, so that the more successful the sales person is, the greater the incentive to do even better.
- Competitions, preferably involving spouses so that the family supports the sales effort. A prize such as a weekend in Copenhagen for two, for the biggest increase in sales over a three month period, is an example. It need not be expensive, particularly off-season.

In addition to financial incentives, in their various forms, most sales people perform much better if their treatment as individuals satisfies various criteria:

- They are given substantial and up-to-date information on the firm and its products or services.

- They are listened to when they wish to comment on their job and the standards they are expected to maintain.

Sales productivity

Sales productivity is possibly the measure of efficiency that can vary more than any other in a firm, especially a small firm where the management tend to have a dozen things to do at any one time and cannot concentrate for long on sales staff. In one small firm, the actual sales call rate per month was compared with what it should reasonably have been, after taking account of such factors as the time needed to travel from one customer to another. Productivity was 10 per cent, i.e. if a sales reporting and control system was installed, it was likely that sales would increase ten times! In other words the sales staff could have seen ten times as many customers and, on the reasonable assumption that they could be as effective selling to new customers as their present ones, sales would have increased accordingly.

Approaching large companies

Successful selling to large companies seems very problematic to many small businesses, for various reasons.

- The large companies have, and have often exercised, the ability to withhold payment from small firms. Sometimes this arises from a deliberate policy to obtain as much credit as possible, regardless of periods of credit defined in the supplier's terms of trade. This can mean that the large firms are paid with reasonable promptness because the supplies they provide are needed to keep a production facility going but the small firms providing more specialized goods or services are made to wait.
- Alternatively, payment may be delayed because documentation is held up in complicated systems. One small debt passes unnoticed amongst a lot of large ones.
- Large firms have very time-consuming purchasing processes, which mean the small firm has to spare someone to make a whole series

of visits, before there is any prospect of an order. If, say, four people are involved in a purchasing decision, each can leave the papers in his 'in tray' for a fortnight before considering the matter.

- It can be puzzling for the representative of a small firm, trying to find out who actually decides what is to be bought and from whom.

On the other hand, large firms often find it convenient to buy from small ones.

- They can deal with one person who not only understands the total operation of his firm but can make things happen.
- The small firm can react more quickly.
- The small firm will be interested in small orders that larger firms would prefer to ignore. For example, a manufacturing company may wish to build a pilot plant for a new process and will find it much easier to buy customized small-scale plant from a small workshop.
- A large firm will often prefer to sustain this kind of relationship, once it is established. Reliability of supply will be much more important than price.

Influencers, recommenders, buyers and order placers

Approaching a large firm is easier if the small one understands that there are often a number of people involved in the buying decision. These can be separated into several categories.

Influencers These are people who are consulted because of their status, expertise, length of service or personality but who do not either recommend the purchase, or actually place the order. One small firm was trying to sell adhesives to a large engineering company. Its representative was always courteously received by the buyer and his technical advisers but three meetings in two months seemed to produce no progress towards an order. Eventually the salesman's manager decided to accompany him on another visit. Once arrived and introduced to the buyer he asked, as a comparative stranger, how the adhesive buying processes worked in the company. The buyer explained that he had a budget which would cover the adhesives, if bought, and was advised by technicians. Before a product could be placed on the firm's list it had to pass tests in a particular laboratory. When pressed, the buyer admitted that the head of this laboratory had been with the firm for 40 years and was almost a law unto himself. As retirement approached, it was obviously easier not to test new suppliers' products and take the risk that they might have some fault, which evaded test scrutiny but which could cause trouble on the production line. Fortunately, a meeting was arranged immediately with this 'influencer' and the aspiring sellers were able to talk technicalities with him to his satisfaction. The product was tested, accepted and bought.

Recommenders These can be in any part of the firm: accountants, product designers, production engineers, technical advisers.

Buyers In the sense of people who decide to buy, the decision takers may be far removed from the buying department. They may be senior executives or directors.

Order placers These may also be called 'buyers'. They will have as close colleagues progress chasers, who may place follow-up orders.

Avoid the mistake of assuming that each of these people has a good knowledge of how his firm works. This may not be the case at all. If a good relationship is established, the sales person from the outside may come to know some parts of the customer company better than some of his contacts. Finally, ensure that a comprehensive list of all the firms' sites is obtained. One of them may hide an independent buyer.

Some large firms have published buying directories, designed to help sales people approach them. They reason that if they make selling easier, they will obtain more worthwhile buying opportunities. Any small firm approaching a large one should ask for this information, whether or not it is readily available.

Payment processes

If sales are subsequently achieved, the new customer should be asked for detailed information about payment processes. Buyers are often very receptive to this kind of request because suppliers complain to them, in the first instance, if they do not get paid when they expect to be. Terms of trade are one thing but actual payment can be quite different. In one case I presented an invoice to a managing director who authorized immediate payment. Some weeks later the payment had not arrived and I pursued the matter within his accounts department. The financial controller told me the matter was 'in hand' but I telephoned again the same day and asked for the person who actually drew the cheques and obtained signatures on them. (Large firms will control expenditure partly by restricting signatories of company cheques to very few people.) She told me she had a departmental instruction to keep all payment-authorized invoices in a file for a month, before starting the signing process – which could take a week. Once I drew her attention to the managing director's instructions, she apologized and I received the cheque a few days later.

Selling for resale

In some circumstances, a small business will sell to a few distributors, rather than a large number of customers. It is easy to think that the selling task has been simplified and the main effort can be concentrated on matters such as design and production. In fact selling has been delegated to other organizations, which may be very supportive but will not identify with the supplying firm's interests as closely as that firm itself. It is selling through distributors rather than to distributors.

Once regular selling of this kind has been established, attention has to be given to sales development, for which information is required. While the distributor will know his customers better than his supplier, the latter will know more about his or her own products. The object of the exercise is to generate more sales by combining the two strengths effectively. This concept often has to be 'sold' to the distributor, probably by a gradual process of making constructive suggestions rather than suggesting a grand plan in the course of one visit. When these suggestions are made depends on the relationship between representatives of supplier and distributor, bearing in mind that the respect of the distributor is more important than cheerful friendliness.

It is easiest if the supplier's representative has a clear view of the information he needs and the information he can provide. The information he needs will be sales information product by product, customer by customer – or at least by groups of distributor customer. The information he should provide will include the way his products are being used by other customers and also what types of business they are. This may make it possible to suggest to the distributor:

- new types of customer to approach;
- new ways of giving their customers reasons to buy.

For example, a small manufacturer of health foods selling through distributors could learn from one distributor the arguments that proved most effective in selling, and thus encourage other distributors to use them. If one of his distributors was particularly successful in selling, not only to grocers but also to chemists/pharmacists and department stores, then that information could be used to encourage other distributors. The twin objectives with distributors would be to help them to achieve the following.

- Sell all, or at least more, of the products in the manufacturer's range. This can be difficult for a distributor who has a long list of products to sell from a number of suppliers. The danger is that he will simply become an order taker. The solution from the manufacturer's point of view is to run promotions, product by product, to get them into retail outlets where they can be sold and orders can be stimulated. Promotions might, for example, combine incentives to the distributor's representatives with a slightly enhanced margin for the retailer – financed by the manufacturer.
- Sell to more customers, as long as those customers were not already being supplied by another of the manufacturer's distributors.

Key points

- Salesmen are made not born.
- Asking good questions is as important a sales skill as producing answers.
- Always ask for the order.
- Make a proposition to the customer and avoid giving too many alternatives to choose from.

10

Selling: Recruiting, advertising and promotion

Outline

Selling can also include:

- hiring sales people – the sequence is described from seeking application to starting the successful candidate on his first day at work
- sales promotion
- advertising and public relations
- sponsorship

The recruitment problem

The recruitment of a sales person to a small firm can be a problem. Large firms can analyse the performance of many sales people, looking for common qualities amongst their more successful people. They may have various aptitude tests to apply and candidates can be interviewed by two or three managers, whose collective judgement can prevent many mistakes. Large firms can find it easier, because of their status and reputation, to attract good applicants. On the other hand, good sales people in large firms are not necessarily effective in smaller ones. Large firms will certainly be more likely to spend management time in devising and applying sales training programmes but their people are more likely to need such support. They will probably be encouraged to join because of the camaraderie of the sales force. Large company sales staff often have large phone bills, not so much because they are telephoning customers but because they are telephoning each other to share the experiences of the day and obtain mutual encouragement.

Small firm advantages

The small firm looking for sales people does have advantages that it can offer.

- Access to the boss. Many larger company sales staff see their local manager on a personal basis but not the more senior management, except in large gatherings at stage-managed morale-boosting meetings.
- Less form filling. The more remote the top management of an organization, the more it needs paper (or computer transmitted information) to find out what is going on.
- More genuine representation of firms. Small company sales people are better informed and have more control over their firms' response to customer interests.
- More responsibility for the whole firm's success. A large firm can carry an unsuccessful sales person, at least for a few months. A small firm cannot afford to.
- Opportunities to compete for success, less by attracting attention in comparison with their colleagues and more by building a business. This can be much more satisfying.

Recruitment preparation

You need to begin any recruitment of sales people by 'selling' your firm and its products or services to candidates, presenting its virtues in a clear and positive way. There are precautions to be taken before recruitment.

- Decide exactly what the new sales person will be responsible for, in terms of area, products and targets.
- Decide how the newcomer will be inducted in matters such as product knowledge, sales and ordering procedures, customer records.
- Choose a good title for the job. People like to tell their friends they have an important sounding position. However, any title that is chosen should genuinely describe the work. A sales person masquerading as a 'sales director' will soon be found out, but 'business development manager' can be perfectly accurate.

- Decide how the new job holder is to be paid in terms of basic salary – setting high and low limits – other incentives and benefits (such as a car).

Recruitment sources can include:

- advertising in local papers, possibly national papers and probably trade journals (you may need people who already know the trade, if you cannot afford the longer learning period of those from other occupations);
- personnel agencies, who will have substantial fees but can be a considerable help in supplying short lists of suitable candidates;
- acquaintances, although popular nephews do not always make good employees!
- employees who want to 'get out on the road';
- people who may have written in asking for sales positions.

Any advertisement or vacancy notice issued to an agency should state clearly what the position is, with whom, how it will be remunerated and what experience is looked for. Remuneration should aim to be competitive – and agencies will advise on this – but protect the business by including a strong payment by results content. Applicants, from all sources, should be asked to submit brief details of their interests, previous work – particularly sales achievements – age and education (although education is not often very important in selecting sales staff). Specifying age limits is still legal in Britain, unlike the United States, but they should not be too precise. People rarely conform to preconceptions about age and ability. Sometimes there is a preference for using box numbers but candidates tend to reply more frequently to advertisements that give precise employer information. A newspaper will usually give assistance with advertisement design – because they want it to reflect well on their publication – and a good agency will certainly advise on the vacancy notice.

Assessing applications

Once received, applications should be studied for qualities that are more likely to bring good sales results.

- Effective selling experience – not just holding a sales job.
- An ability to sell him or herself on paper, without implausible exaggeration.
- The traditional sales qualities of integrity and a willingness to work hard. Integrity does matter if you are going to trust him or her with part of your business future.
- Evidence of an ability to go out and make things happen. Someone who produces the village pantomime is more likely to be a good sales person than someone who watches plays.
- Ambition, the desire to move on to a better position. Good sales people are mobile and positive. This does not necessarily mean that they will use a small firm just as a stepping stone, although two years of a good sales person is often better than ten years of an indifferent one. In any case ambition can often be accommodated within a single firm, even a small one, by offering increasing rewards and status – as long as they are matched by increasing achievement.

Interviewing

If possible three or four candidates should be interviewed. Five interviews will involve too much repetition and the risk of hazy judgement. Two gives too little choice and, if one drops out, none at all. The timing of interviews matters. Concentration declines in the early and late afternoon. The candidate who seems least suited should be interviewed first, so that the interviewers can accustom themselves to the job. A second interviewer can be a great help, a colleague or even, for part of the time, another sales person. Two heads are better than one, particularly when making judgements about people.

Overall the interviewers should be talking for about one-third of the time, the candidate for the rest of the time. The interview should begin with one of the interviewers explaining how the business operates, so that the candidate can relax. He should be invited to ask questions and then be questioned about his career so far. Eventually, he should be asked what his ambitions are, why the job appeals to him and why he thinks he is suited.

In deciding which of the candidates should be offered the post, the temptation should be resisted to rush to a decision. Certainly, the post should not be offered during the interview, although there are occasions when first impressions are correct. Even if they are, the interview procedure should be followed because the candidate will think more of the firm if this is done. If the candidate says he has other interesting offers – one of the most frequently used means that candidates employ to force a decision, the answer should be to say that in his interests as well as the firm's the decision will be carefully considered. An offer to telephone as soon as that decision is taken should be made. If the candidate is a genuine sales person he or she will use sales methods in the interview (asking questions, overcoming objections, etc.) and his doing so should strengthen his application.

In some cases it is highly desirable that a decision is made quickly, immediately after the last interview. One candidate for a sales job was very impressed, when he arrived home from an interview, to find that the firm had telephoned and asked that he return the call as soon as he returned. He did so and was offered the job, subject to references. If a candidate is unsuccessful, he should still be told, either

- that the post is being offered to another candidate but that he has been placed on a reserve list and will be contacted later to tell him the outcome – it is too early to make a firm commitment, the winner might turn the job down, or his references could be unsatisfactory; or
- that they appreciated his coming to see them but it has been decided to offer the post to another candidate.

This promptness in telling candidates the outcome can only enhance the firm's reputation. Unsuccessful candidates might be encouraged to apply again on another occasion, when they might be better suited to the vacancy at that time.

Deciding who to select and making the offer

Taking the employment decision is most easily done, if the candidates are ranked in order of preference. In doing this, account should be taken of the various qualities required, particularly effective selling experience, but instinct and hunch should never be ignored. It is so important in small firms that a newcomer should 'fit', that is the employer should feel at ease with him. This judgement may be disproved with experience, but that is an insufficient reason for relying on pure logic when the appointment is being considered.

Having telephoned the successful candidate and assuming he does not turn down the offer, a confirming letter should follow. This letter not only makes a contractual offer, it should serve to reinforce the good impression that hopefully has been created. It should include:

- The offer, using phrases such as: 'Thank you for coming to see us on . . . We are pleased to offer you an appointment as . . ., subject to satisfactory references.'
- The duties and the person to whom the appointee will report. This last point is very important. Small firms have a reputation for being dangerously vague in this area. Statements like 'You will report to the directors' can drive a good man away. The old saying applies: 'No man can serve two masters.' The fear is that contradictory instructions can be received from two directors, which can make the employee feel like the rope in a tug-of-war.
- The pay and benefits.
- The means by which the applicant will be inducted into his new duties and the time that will be set aside for it.
- The length of the contract, i.e. the period of notice. The employer may wish to begin with a one-month contract, extending to three months after six months in the job, if the appointee's work is satisfactory. A three-month contract can be a significant liability to a small firm but it can also be an asset. It protects the firm from losing the services of an important employee before he or she can be replaced.
- A request for the names, appointments, addresses and telephone numbers of two referees. One should normally be the present or most recent employer but the applicant may not, for reasons that do not reflect on his suitability for the new post, be on good terms with that employer and may wish to substitute someone else who has knowledge of his sales experience.

Using referees

The function of referees is to help reduce the possibility of a mistaken appointment. Most people approached in this capacity are pleased to do so. Being invited to offer opinions on other people is an implied form of flattery! Contacting referees should not be undertaken hastily. It is a form of insurance.

Most employers prefer to do so by phone. Leaving it to a letter takes longer and relies much more on the ability of the referee to understand what is required. Before picking up the phone, a few minutes thought should be given to the questions to be asked, remembering that the object of the exercise is to find out how likely it is that the potential appointee will be successful in his new post, not necessarily how successful he is in his present position. After all, it may be that he is leaving it because he took lots of orders and the firm failed to deliver many of them.

Often it helps to tell the referee something of the new position and the qualities required, so that he can comment accordingly. In a small firm particularly, a salesman will probably be in a position of trust and this can be checked with both referees.

One of the reasons for having two referees is that every individual has a slightly different view of another individual. Different people see different virtues and vices in the same person.

If the references are satisfactory, the appointee should be telephoned and a starting date (assuming he still wishes to go ahead) agreed. A confirming letter should follow, specifying the starting date, time and place and to whom he should report on arrival, also any documentation he should bring with him, such as tax papers. Written confirmation of acceptance should be requested.

The first day

Firms often spoil good impressions at the selection stage, by giving the employee a casual reception on his first day at work. He is of course an investment, costing money as soon as he walks in the door. The more effectively he is taught what he needs to know, to do the job, the sooner will a return on that investment start to accrue. He is much more likely to identify quickly with the firm's interests if he is given a timetabled plan on arrival, leading to active selling in the near future.

Small businesses seldom have time to produce such plans on paper and it is easier if the employer has simply decided the main phases of the induction programme and the time by which they should be completed. A good sales person will arrive with some ideas on what he wants to do in the early stages and this too makes the process easier.

When the sales person arrives, you should aim to cover the following points.

- The people to meet in the firm and what they do.
- Briefing on the products, usually by means of a price list, if this was not done adequately at the interview stage.
- The customers, how and where they are listed.
- How the ordering, delivering and invoicing functions operate.
- The date by which he should aim to complete his initial familiarization.
- Who will introduce him to his first customers.
- When he is expected to start selling on his own.

This programme should be short. If he starts at the beginning of the week, he should have met his first customer by the end of the week. Many good sales people become restless if they are kept in the office or factory for too long.

Personal presentation

Some thought should be given to the way a sales person presents him or herself, when visiting customers. For example, one small firm insisted on clean cars, to the point that their sales manager used to inspect them regularly. One salesman failed the inspection because, although the exterior was clean and shining, the engine compartment was dirty. However, this is an extreme example! (If a sales person has a dirty car, it should be parked well away from the customer's premises.)

Not only should the sales person arrive in a reasonably smart manner, his equipment should impress without being too slick. He should carry it in a good case (or cases) and it should be organized so that it can be produced quickly when needed. Fumbling for a price list can destroy any good impression that has been built up by the previous part of the presentation. One sales manager carried a video camera when visiting distributors, just in case it might be needed. At one call, he explained how he thought his products should be sold, treating the distributor as a 'dummy' customer. The distributor was so impressed he asked if he could use it to train his sales people. The sales manager repeated the presentation, this time with the video running, then handed over the tape to the highly satisfied distributor. Within a year that distributor had increased his sales of the sales manager's products by 500 per cent.

In most circumstances the sales person needs the following items.

- Standard documentation such as order pads and perhaps receipt forms, if he is collecting cash.
- That customer's records.
- A planning form, so that he can suggest quantities to the buyer, without the buyer feeling he is being forced too soon to make up his mind. When the order is agreed it can be transferred to the order form.
- A diary/notebook.
- Product information. These can be presented in a number of ways: samples if they are small enough to be carried; illustrations which should be carried in a folder of transparent sleeves; video kits. The latter are expensive and heavy. However, they can be very effective in that they guarantee a professional presentation, which allows the salesman to relax and concentrate his attention on the customer without worrying about his own materials.

Retail sales staff

There is one very large group of sales people in small businesses who frequently receive, at least in the United Kingdom, less recognition and training than seems appropriate. Retail sales staff are often described as shop assistants – no mention of selling in the title. Yet they often carry the reputation of the smaller shops with them. The term shop assistant implies a passive role, doing such work as the manager or owner directs. This naturally affects the way most shop staff work, which comes down to a process of taking money, wrapping some of the purchases and answering a few questions from customers. It makes for a weary day.

The job can be much more interesting than that, provided some responsibility is given to the 'shop assistant' and, preferably, his or her job described differently – perhaps as sales staff, or salesman or saleswoman. For example, in a CTN (confectioner, tobacconist, newsagent) a sales person might be given responsibility for the confectionery side, in addition to serving customers generally. These special responsibilities could be as follows:

- Checking stock and telling the manager when reordering is necessary and how much should be reordered of each size and brand.
- Refilling shelves and displays from the stock room.
- Price labelling the product.
- Rearranging displays to increase sales. This can often be done by placing the best-selling items where the customers are most likely to notice them, such as next to the best selling-newspapers, or where they will be noticed as customers wait to pay for other items they have bought. Using manufacturers' display material to advantage. Creating own-display material, e.g. stencilled placards on the shelving with names and prices of new products.
- Encouraging hesitant customers to buy from the confectionery sections of the shop, e.g. 'Our Easter eggs came in yesterday.'

This change of role would mean more specific training for the sales person, in stock checking and in display. It would also mean recruiting possibly a more outgoing type of person, who could make the right buying suggestions to customers and feel confident in doing so.

In addition to effective selling, there are a variety of techniques that can be used to increase sales. Rather than start with a list of examples, it is more helpful to consider the main types.

Sales promotion

Sales promotion means changing temporarily the value offered to the customer, so that more people will try the product or service, in the expectation that some will be permanently converted to it. An example of this technique is a restaurant that offers reduced prices, on a selection from its menu, to customers ordering before a certain time in the evening, say 7 p.m. It hopes that the new customers will return on other evenings to order after 7 p.m. when prices are higher. A delicatessen may invite customers to sample a new cheese. A book store may reduce prices of second-hand books for a limited period, if two or more are bought together.

Sales promotions should never be established with the vague aim of 'boosting sales'. Objectives should be set and performance measured against them (e.g. 20 per cent increase in sales of promoted item), although this can be more difficult than it seems. A restaurant with reduced menu prices in the early evening may experience an upsurge in trade that is caused by fine weather in an early spring, as well as by the promotion. The delicatessen would need to compare sales of

- the cheeses sampled;
- other cheeses;
- all other products – because attracting people into the store to try the cheese may cause them to notice and buy other products that have nothing to do with cheese.

Measurement should be continued for some time after the promotion, so that the natural falling-off of sales of the promoted products can be noted.

A variant of the principle of giving free samples of a product successfully is demonstrated by a firm which invented a new kind of speciality chemical which, when used in photo-processing, reduced over-all costs. Potential customers were sceptical and unwilling to risk spending money without proof that it would actually reduce costs. The supplier was so confident that it would easily pay for itself that he offered to supply, on a free trial basis, with payment later if the product claims were proved. Invariably they were.

Exhibitions

Exhibitions and product demonstrations can be useful to small businesses, especially on an individual basis. Trade customers are invited to a hotel room, where goods can be displayed together with promotional literature. One or more employees attend to encourage interest and explain the products or services. Only modest hospitality is required, such as coffee or tea. The advantage lies not only in the opportunity to sell but also in the chance to attract new contacts, who when known can serve to extend the customer base. They may not buy immediately but the new opportunity is there. Many hotels are thoroughly accustomed to arranging this kind of event, which need not be particularly expensive.

Advertising

Advertising is inherently more wasteful than most sales promotion because it is difficult to target the message as precisely as with sales promotion. Often advertising is not so much intended to sell directly but to help people to remember the product, so that when they see the product, in a store for example, they are more likely to buy. Sometimes advertising has very long-term objectives, like the car advertisements which are read mainly by people who already own them and find sufficient reassurance to want to buy the same make again.

On the other hand, advertising is often much easier to arrange than an ongoing sales promotion. The cheaper media, such as local and trade newspapers, cinema and local radio frequently value small businesses as a growth opportunity and make it easier for them to advertise. Stills for advertisers can be shown in the cinema with a voice-over giving the advertising message. Radio is even easier, as a simple tape recorder is the only tool needed. However, you still need to consider:

- to whom you wish to send the message;
- exactly what that message will be.

Some media, like some local newspapers, have access to more people than others do. People who are at home during the day may well listen to local radio, while the working under 35s are more likely to go to the cinema in the evening. Both of these media should be asked to describe their audience in fairly precise terms before any time is booked.

Evaluating advertising

If advertising is used, an attempt should be made to evaluate the effect. One gas fitter obtained a certificate of technical proficiency and received free advertising in local newspapers from the certifying authority. After two years of free advertising he surprised them by asking that his name be removed because the only business it had ever brought him had been emergency calls at the end of the week when the fault was a small one. He decided that he preferred a quiet Friday evening at home to the occasional low-fee job.

If you have analysed the strengths and other qualities, as described in chapter 6, you will find it easier to compose an advertising message. It should have various characteristics:

- Memorability – a fairly short and easy trading name helps, especially one that is not in common use. Two syllable names are best. Some people remember what they hear, in which case two very distinct syllables, such as Broadgate, are important for radio advertising; others remember what they see and an unusual name such as Sincrown can be effective in press advertising.
- A clear statement of the product's particular claims to equality with, if not superiority over, its competitors.
- Clear information as to how the product can be bought. It is surprising how often this information is tucked away in small print.

The advertisement itself should be designed so as to attract attention and carry conviction.

It is a feature of advertising that it is competing with other attractions, or distractions, for attention. Memory fades unless it is used with some frequency. There is the story of a manufacturer of a well-advertised and very well-known product. On a long train journey he was approached by a stranger who asked why he did not save money by stopping advertising. He replied by asking why the railway company did not save money by uncoupling the engine and letting the train carry on on its own. It was after all travelling at a steady 80 miles per hour. His point was that advertising has to be continued, if it is to remain effective.

Advertising can be used without media by delivering direct to the audience, by direct mail (which can involve arranging reply-paid letters or cards with the postal services) or on a house-to-house basis. The latter can be particularly attractive to small businesses because of the modest amount of work involved. A leaflet can be drafted and design and printing handled by a local printer. Delivery can be arranged with a free newspaper distributor, for example. Again it is important to have clear, obtainable objectives and to target properly.

This type of promotional activity might well have saved a small shoe retailing and repair business, which closed recently in a big city suburb. The business had provided the local community with good service, to consistent quality standards, for 40 years, and the proprietor was puzzled when he heard, from time to time, of local residents being unaware of what he had to offer. Unfortunately, the number of people who knew about the business was shrinking, as residents died or moved away, but no attempt was made to bring his message home to those who replaced them, beyond the presence of his shop on a shopping parade. His prices were highly competitive but that was not enough. The business satisfied three of the criteria of good marketing: good products, in a good place, at good prices. The fourth criterion, good promotion, was missing.

A more sophisticated form of leaflet is the kind used to give potential customers information on products. It can vary from a single page price list to a multi-page leaflet, with photographs and drawings of products and detailed information. These can be expensive but necessary if the product is complex. Its detail will remind of essential information and, if it is well designed and printed, it is more likely to command respect. More than one small business has moved from zero turnover to more than £1m, by means of good leafleting.

Sponsorship

Sponsorship is becoming more and more popular as a means of promotion. No longer is it confined to large firms spending large sums of money to be associated, for instance, with major sporting events. Local firms, known mainly to their customers, can now make their names known to a much wider public by associating themselves with an event or an organization. A music shop can sponsor a performance by a local orchestra. A small engineering company can sponsor one of the home matches of the local football team. A toy shop can sponsor an infant play school. In each case there is publicity in front of the right kind of audience if that publicity is arranged appropriately. The music shop will have its name published in a prominent position on the programme: it may even arrange an exhibition of music and instruments before the concert and during the interval. The engineering company will have its name, as sponsor, on a board visible from outside the football ground the week before the match, as well as having the sponsorship publicized in the programme. The infant play school will have a prominent notice informing parents of the sponsorship, and the information may well be included in any communications to the parents.

Managing sponsorship

Sponsorship is not charity. It is business. Therefore it needs to be defined in detail, in writing, to avoid misunderstandings. The music shop, for example, would need to specify

- the date, place and time of the concert and details of the programme (if the shop sells a lot of wind instruments, it would not serve their purpose to sponsor a programme consisting entirely of piano and string pieces);
- the precise manner and position in which their name would appear on the programme;
- the location and size of the area set aside for their exhibition;
- other considerations, such as lighting and early access to set it up;
- payments to be made, the amount and timing.

Other sponsorship contracts could be much more detailed. The engineering company could have a particular typographical design for the company name on the outside of its workshop, which it would wish to see reproduced on the football club board, so that it would be recognized more easily by local people, who might visit it as potential employees or customers.

As with promotion the objectives should be clear to the sponsoring company: sales to the music shop and the toy shop; perhaps ease of recruiting as well as sales to the engineering company. The extent to which these had been achieved should be measured over an appropriate period. The toy shop sponsorship might be monitored for a year, for example.

Careful checks should be made to ensure that the conduct and situation of the sponsored organization are consistent with the interests of the sponsors. It would not help the toy shop if the play school was short of children and threatened with closure. Nor would it benefit the engineering company if four players had been sent off in a match earlier in the season.

Public relations

A major potential weapon in even the small business person's armoury is public relations. The essence of public relations is obtaining third party approval. Although the gas fitter did not want to advertise on a list of approved fitters, he was glad to have it on his invoices so that he could claim that form of third party approval as an endorsement of his expertise. The retailer who pays a television celebrity to open his new shop is using the same technique, so is a restaurant that can claim a place in one of the prestige guides. Frequently, public relations involves finding out what the media, such as local press and radio, are interested in publicizing. A publican who took over and refurbished a 400-year-old public house, after a career in the oil industry all over the world, found the local press were only too pleased to attend the opening and publish his story. They had a newspaper to fill and were glad of genuine help, in a story that they judged their readers would like to see.

Handling bad publicity

The reverse of seeking publicity for a good story is being ready to answer questions when bad news breaks. Hiding is no remedy, nor is 'no comment'. It is in the interest of the business to reduce the damage to its reputation as much as possible, as soon as possible. For example, the restaurant that receives an adverse report from a health inspector must demonstrate that it is taking immediate action to restore hygiene standards – and say what they are.

This process of being ready to answer questions has the following meaning.

- Considering what the questions are likely to be, particularly hostile questions. Fairness will not necessarily be uppermost in the minds of local journalists.
- Preparing answers that are factual but at the same time give information that shows the business in a more favourable light.
- Being aware that journalists have deadlines to meet. The less time they have to prepare reports, the less likely are their reports to be accurate. Luck is an important element in the process. Bad news breaking on a Thursday afternoon for a local newspaper, which publishes on a Friday, can receive headline treatment because it is so recent and yet contain inaccuracies because of the haste of reporting and subediting. If that news breaks on a Friday morning it may never appear in that newspaper.

Newspapers, and particularly radio and television stations, are increasingly in the habit of using the 'news bite' as more and more items are crammed into the same time or space. A news bite is a short answer to the question that editors judge to be of greatest interest to the viewing or reading public. Therefore it is very important to put the right message across. If the first questions are: 'Is it true that the authorities are prosecuting for a breach of health regulations? If so what are they complaining of?' and they are answered by: 'Yes. They found cockroaches', the publicity will be much worse than if the answer is: 'The kitchen has been cleaned by pest control experts and we shall be serving our customers this evening. The pests have gone.' The problem is not denied but it is put into a much more favourable context.

Ideally a relationship will have been established with the local press when the business has used promotions to attract good publicity but this will not always be the case.

Giving to charity

A modest charity budget can be helpful. Local organizations can be very important to a small business. A branch of a charity which looks after the elderly would be well disposed towards a local retailer who made an annual donation. This would be particularly relevant if the business needed the custom of local old age pensioners, who found travel to the nearest supermarket inconvenient. A residents association could be particularly helpful, if a business was threatened by a planning application for a road widening scheme. Many small businesses need the goodwill of their local community and charitable donations can help sustain it. Gifts of redundant stock are often welcome, which reduces the actual cost.

Key points

- In a small firm, hiring the right sales person can be critical. Time should be allowed to do it thoroughly.
- Sales promotion concentrates on what is likely to make customers buy.
- Advertising needs less work but involves more waste because its message is scattered more widely.
- Sponsorship and public relations are as practical and as useful for the small firm as they are for the large one.
- Know how to handle bad news as well as good news.

11

Buying and selling: Successful negotiating

Outline

Negotiating skills are described and they include:

- preparation
- listening and questioning
- trading concessions
- avoiding misunderstanding
- maintaining the momentum of negotiation

The meaning of negotiation

Negotiating involves recognizing situations where the terms of trade can be changed to one's advantage. In the industrialized West many buyers accept the authority of the price and wait for temporary reductions, if they can. However, there is the case of an immigrant from the Far East who settled in the West with his family and visited the local family owned supermarket on a Saturday morning to buy groceries. He filled his trolley and moved to the check-out. To the cashier's surprise he did not just deposit his purchases by the till and wait for them to be listed. Every time he picked one of the groceries up he nominated a price that was below the store's price. The cashier was astonished and rang her bell for the owner, who arrived quickly. Then it was the immigrant's turn to be astonished. He could not imagine a trading system where there was no negotiation. Fortunately for him the owner entered into the spirit of the occasion and the two began a weekly process of negotiating over groceries. The owner quickly exploited his strengths – the next supermarket was several miles away – and soon achieved his usual profit margins, sometimes getting an above-listed price sometimes below. The two became firm friends.

Negotiating from ignorance

Sometimes negotiating advantage can be derived from ignorance. A chemicals company sent a highly qualified salesman to see a buyer in a pharmaceuticals firm, to discuss a possible order for a bulk chemical. The chemicals firm was not at that time a supplier but hoped to become one. On the day the salesman arrived, the buyer was ill and a senior chemist in the research and development division was asked to see him instead. The salesman explained that he could offer a substantial discount on the normal price for a first shipment of 2 tonnes. The research executive was uninhibited by purchasing experience and he asked for the same discount to be applied for a two-year period, during which consumption of the chemical would be 50 tonnes. The salesman asked to use a telephone privately and came back into the room to say that his sales director had agreed the discount for two years. The researcher was disappointed to receive only a note of thanks from the head of the buying department and not a salary bonus!

Negotiating to overcome a refusal to sell

There can be occasions when the potential buyer wants to buy something that is not apparently for sale. He should take heart from the experience of a businessman who decided that a particular industrial site would be ideal for his business, even though there was a busy workshop already there. He telephoned the owner and said that he would like to buy the lease (having estimated that it was worth £50,000). The owner replied abruptly that it was not for sale, so the businessman responded: 'Do you mean that if I offered you £100,000 for the lease, you would not take it?' The owner replied: 'That is different'; and the businessman countered by saying: 'In which case it is for sale and you and I are simply talking about the price.' Negotiations began and the lease changed hands for £48,000.

Preparing for negotiation

Before entering into a negotiating process, a general appreciation should be made of the situation.

- What are the comparative strengths and needs of the parties in respect of this particular issue? This does not mean that negotiation should not be attempted with a much larger firm. It may itself be under pressure, perhaps to reduce its stocks, or it may be a firm of commercial estate agents which has had a property you want on its books for longer than its principals would like.
- How urgent is the matter, for you and for them? By when do you need to conclude the matter and what deadline do you judge they have in mind?
- How important is it for you? Does it involve enough money to make it worth your while negotiating? Negotiation is a process which requires special preparation, so most small businesses can only afford to pick out a few major sales or purchases and approach them in this way. Such items might include wage negotiations, a new lease for premises or a new machine for a workshop.

Consideration of these points should make it easier to decide whether to try and negotiate. Negotiation occurs when two parties have a mutual interest in agreement but differ as to the precise nature of that agreement. If the maximum that one party is prepared to offer is below the minimum that another party is prepared to accept, there is no basis for an agreement. This situation sometimes occurs in an industrial dispute and it drags on until one or both of the parties alters its expectations and negotiations begin.

List the negotiating points

The next task in preparing for negotiation is to list (often mentally but written down if the list is a long one) the points that one hopes to gain or the points that represent the limits to which you will go . For a machine for a workshop, these might include the following.

- Total purchase price of £9000.
- £7000 invoiced one month after delivery.
- Remaining £2000 invoiced two months after delivery.
- Payment due 60 days after invoicing.
- Supplier's engineer to assist with installation, on day of delivery, and test run machine to customer's satisfaction.
- Two-year guarantee.
- When guarantee expires, a labour and spares maintenance agreement.
- A two-hour response from the supplier in the event of machine breakdown.
- Evening delivery and installation so that the daytime work of producing to meet customer orders is unimpeded.
- Delivery on a date to be nominated by the customer. Time is an important variable in any negotiation, witness the employers who concede a percentage wage increase in return for an agreement that it shall extend over 18 months rather than a year.
- Compensation if delivery delayed, of £100 a day.
- Change of specification.

Anticipating the supplier's negotiating points

In his sales presentation, the supplier may well have given his terms and presented them as fixed. These could cover

- total purchase price of £10,000;
- 10 per cent deposit payable with order;
- remainder of purchase price invoiced on delivery and payable within 30 days;
- one-year guarantee;
- delivery date to be notified when deposit payment completed.

Other facilities that the supplier might be prepared to consider have to be estimated. They might include

- change of specification;
- his best efforts to give more specific notice of delivery;
- annual service agreements when the guarantee has expired.

Determining the negotiating strategy

The next stage of preparation is to decide the minimum that will be accepted. This depends on

- the ease with which an alternative source can be used;
- the loss of profit that might accrue from delaying the purchase;
- the time that can be spared from other tasks in the business.

Once this is completed, the customer is in a position to begin negotiation. If possible he should do this in a situation, such as an office, where he is less likely to be distracted. Negotiating on home ground is usually an advantage, especially for a small business person. Not only can you control interruptions but you can begin negotiating when it suits you.

Defeating intimidation

Larger firms in particular have plenty of devices to make the visiting negotiator feel at a disadvantage:

1 Making you wait well beyond the appointed time, perhaps on your own in a small room. There are various ways of countering this tactic, such as:

   - taking work with you and getting on with it, as if the delay is useful and not an inconvenience;
   - asking for a phone so that you can call your business and talk to your employees;
   - asking for more information about the firm you are visiting, such as the names of colleagues of the contact;
   - asking for the use of office facilities, such as photocopiers.

   All these devices can give the impression of a busy and successful business person who has a great deal to do in the working day. They also have the advantage of preventing you from sitting and worrying about the outcome of the negotiation. Your confidence is enhanced and that confidence makes a successful outcome more likely.

2 Holding the meeting in a lavishly furnished conference room.

3 Alternatively, holding it in a small office and allowing frequent

interruptions from colleagues and taking all telephone calls. This is no reason for you to deviate from your objectives.

4 Saying at the beginning of the meeting: 'I can only spare twenty minutes!' I was once subjected to this treatment but took no notice and worked towards my objectives. The meeting ended successfully and amicably an hour and a half later. I reminded the big company executive of his original time limit. It was obvious from his reaction that he had forgotten it and that it was simply a negotiating manoeuvre.

Listening and questioning

Once the negotiations have begun the best general advice is

- listen,
- ask questions.

Listening, particularly when the other party is summarizing its position, gives the opportunity to hear if the other party is changing its position, and they may well do so, simply because a silent attentive audience prompts the desire to talk. Asking questions means, apart from the obvious advantage of acquiring information, using the best technique for dealing with unwelcome propositions. Such questions can also be used to make the other party think more about the implications of their position: 'Do you want our opinions of your machine to be based on our testing it without one of your engineers being present?' This question hints at a possible weakness in their position, which they may not have considered.

Some questions can require specific answers, such as asking for the longest continuous running time any of their customers have obtained from the machine. Others seek to strengthen a position by asking for opinions: 'Do you think your new machine will wear as well as the last one?' The seller cannot deny that he has less experience of it and less information and may be forced to reply with a generality such as: 'We have great confidence in it', which does not improve his negotiating stance.

Sometimes the process of trading concessions can be compressed by asking 'if' questions: 'If we take only 30-days credit, will you deliver by the end of next month?'

Negotiating principles are not just for application in complicated matters. A customer walked into an electrical shop and asked to buy a new kind of telephone. The sales person went away to the stock-room and returned with the information that the product on display was the last in stock. The customer asked for a discount as it was shop soiled. The sales person stood his ground and explained that it was not policy to reduce the price of displayed products, whereupon the customer said he was sure he could find one in another store. The sales person hurriedly returned to the stock-room and returned to say that he had found one after all still in its package. By this time he was so anxious to please this customer that he consulted the company price list and said the price on display was incorrect. The customer left the store with the product he wanted reduced in price by a quarter. By keeping his mind on the objective of the best possible value for money, he did much better than he might have expected if he had not attempted to make his purchase in a negotiating frame of mind. The detail of those negotiations and the surprising change of mind by the sales person are less important than the result.

Avoid objecting

Never make flat objections. The object of the exercise is to continue the negotiation until there is a reasonably satisfactory outcome. An objection halts that process and may generate an emotional response, which makes it all the more difficult to restart. A statement such as: 'We do not offer maintenance agreements', could be countered by: 'What do you say to other customers who must have asked the same question?' which is better than: 'We want one.'

Trading concessions

The heart of the negotiating process is the trading of concessions, which is where the preparation is so valuable. A good list of requirements and a planned willingness to compromise means that offers of concessions can be made to obtain counter-concessions. If a request for evening delivery is made in the knowledge that a late afternoon delivery can be accommodated, then that can be offered as a genuine concession even if the originator does not regard it as such. A concession is a matter primarily of presentation and not necessarily substance. It is used to regain the initiative in an exchange between two individuals, or two groups.

Negotiating with groups

Sometimes you might be confronted by several representatives of the other party. This can be an advantage. If they have rehearsed their presentation and negotiating stance, which does happen but not very often, they can still be placed at a disadvantage by

- reminding one of the individuals of something he has said on a previous occasion, which contradicts what a colleague has said in the meeting;
- directing questions to an individual which only he can answer, for example a technical engineer accompanying a commercial sales person.

These tactics are designed to weaken the other party's case, by making it more likely that they will cease to form a completely united front.

Two's company

There can, nevertheless, be advantages in having a colleague or an adviser present in negotiations, provided his or her role is made completely clear. It is particularly important that he or she takes a secondary role and that your role as decision maker is not compromised. He could be used, for instance, to provide information – in a buying situation – 'on cue' on the performance of competitive equipment.

Rehearsals

The fact that rehearsals are not often used before negotiations, except by trade unions before wage and other negotiations, is a good reason for you to use them before really important negotiations. A rehearsal needs some preparation, including a different briefing paper for each side and the use of a room where your representatives and colleagues, acting the part of the other side, can rehearse without interruption, from the telephone or anything else. If possible there should be at least three people in that room, one of them to act as moderator (or umpire) so that the negotiation has a seriousness and a formality that makes the practice more worth while. If you go into 'real thing' having had many of the awkward counter-arguments thrown at you in practice, you are much better prepared, just as a tennis player going on to the Centre Court at Wimbledon for a match is better prepared if he has 'warmed up' on a practice court. To ensure that the rehearsal does not degenerate into too much informality, either the moderator or the players should conclude the session with a list of what has been agreed.

Maintaining good relations

Often the greatest challenge in negotiation is retaining good relationships with the other party, which is important if a harmonious long-term trading association is desired. An intention to negotiate does not imply hostility but the exchange does need to be handled with positive respect for the expertise of the other party. However, in many parts of the world a trader who does not negotiate *loses* respect because he has taken the fun out of it. I have sat in on a negotiation between a Chinese factory owner in Malaysia and his customer. They made proposals and counter-proposals, laughing for most of the time, about a small consignment of rubber where the difference between them was never more than 20 pence!

Using absent friends

While it is always desirable in negotiations to aim to conclude the deal in a single discussion, there can be circumstances where one party needs a breathing space to reconsider his position. The way to handle this is to refer to the need to talk to someone who is not present. With a large firm this is easily done by referring to a more senior executive in the business but you need not be deterred. You can for instance say: 'I need to check this with my workshop foreman' (or accountant, or lawyer). This confirms your seriousness while relieving the pressure.

Take a break

Another way of relieving the pressure if need be is to take a break in the proceedings, on the pretext of leaving the room to check that something is being done by colleagues, or make an urgent call on a family matter, which rarely causes resentment.

One negotiator used to arrange these informal breaks so that he could contrive to see the other party outside the room, when he could refer to an outstanding point of difference and quickly suggest a compromise. Taking a break can also allow more time to think about and assess the other party's true motives, if these are not easy to discern. They might be one or more of a number of alternatives:

- A desire to feel important, be in control, or just protest once during the exchange. In which case satisfy this desire by a rapid concession on a point that is more important to him than to you.
- Excessive reliance on reasoning and lingering over detail. If the other party wants to enjoy the process, let him. Just concentrate on the main objectives.

Sudden concessions

Sometimes the other party can disarm a negotiator with the sudden offer of a major concession. The one who benefits instinctively suspects he has missed some disadvantage but he may miss the opportunity to conclude the negotiation by suspicious hesitation. The correct reaction is to repeat the concession to make sure it was properly understood.

In a precision engineering firm, the trade union was conducting annual wage negotiations with management. These negotiations had focused on a percentage increase in the basic hourly rates of pay, and the previous evening the management had offered an increase of 5 per cent, which was rejected. Considerable overtime was worked in the small factory at separately determined rates, which were not at that point the subject of negotiation. In fact the union felt they were already generous and that they would have to settle for a lesser overtime percentage increase than the 5 per cent they had rejected for basic rates. To their surprise the management reopened the negotiations by offering a 7 per cent increase on total pay. The other side were fairly certain that this was a slip of the tongue, by comparatively inexperienced management, but kept a straight face and repeated what had just been offered. The offer was confirmed. The trade union side responded by thanking the management for their constructive attitude and expressed pleasure that the annual negotiations would probably be concluded without industrial action of any kind, once they had reported back to their members.

Using history

Where there is already a history of contact between the parties, that history may include situations where there was disappointment on one side or the other, perhaps because of a late delivery. This is a definite negotiating point because it can be offered as a counter-question to some requirement of the other party. It is important not to use it in an aggressive manner because that can increase the emotional tone of the discussion and retard progress. Introduce it by reminding the other party of what happened and suggest a remedy. For example: 'We did have difficulties with delivery last time. Perhaps we could check with one of your people this time, a week before. Who should we ask for?' This produces not only the benefit of reducing the likelihood of late delivery but also distracts from their previous demand, which may be forgotten. Even if it is remembered later, it will have to be traded for another concession.

Repeating the agreement

Repeating all the details of what has been agreed, at what seems to be the end of the exchanges, can prove a valuable safety precaution.

All too many negotiations have proved a waste of time and goodwill because one party thought, incorrectly, that he had won a particularly good deal and rushed away while his luck held. Had he kept his nerve and checked his understanding of the arrangement, he might have had to make a concession to conclude the matter but he would still have achieved a result that was much better than a deal resulting from restarted negotiations after the other side rejected, in annoyance, the misunderstood agreement.

Sometimes the device of repeating what has been agreed can be used half-way through the negotiations. A concise summary can even be a relief to the other side and improve the climate of negotiation. It can also give the side making the statement an opportunity to think of more questions.

Despite all these devices and precautions, there may be occasions when negotiations come to a halt because the other party seems to have decided that it has conceded as much as it can. Unless you too want to walk away from the table, there are tactics to deal with even this situation:

- Ask for the situation to be summarized. Staying in the room and seeming calm can impress in itself. It also allows for the possibility that such a summary may result in a change of position, that suits you.
- Express surprise that progress is not being made and invite suggestions.
- If possible make a comparison with a previous agreement on some other occasion and ask what is so different about it that agreement has not been reached on this occasion.

Remembering the lessons

Because a small business does not have the time to engage in too many negotiations, it may be some time before the next one. The danger is that the details of the achievement can be at least partly forgotten, unless some kind of written record is made. This record should emphasize

- what was learned about negotiating;

- what particular approach proved effective with that particular trader.

No two negotiations are ever quite the same but learning by experience is still important.

Although negotiating skill does not appear in the balance sheet, it is an important asset to a business. Wherever possible you should seek to spread your acquired skills amongst partners or colleagues. There can be severe cost penalties if you are preoccupied or ill on negotiating occasions and no adequate substitute is available. The way to pass the skill on is to

- involve the colleague in rehearsals;
- review the results and the short report at the end of each negotiation;
- have your colleague accompany you to negotiations but with a strictly defined role, perhaps to answer questions in a limited area or perhaps simply to meet the other party.

An important point to remember. Do not take yourself too seriously, because the other party will not. A sense of humour equals a sense of proportion and the ability to think more quickly, which is a great asset.

Negotiating repeat purchases

So far the comments on negotiation have focused particularly on the situation of the buyer when negotiating for an expensive single item of capital equipment. Many businesses, of course, do most of their buying for repeat order items, such as food for a restaurant, stationery for a secretarial services agency or simply products for resale.

One man set up a car spares retailing business and found he was confronted with manufacturers' price lists with a scale of discounts that gave great advantage to the multiple chains. His solution was to invite each of the sales people, separately, to meet him away from the business in a cafe or some such suitable place. Once there, he negotiated, equipped with a mental list of all he could offer the big manufacturer. In particular he was able to compare his small one-outlet firm favourably with the multiples who were getting the big discounts, in various ways:

- He personally had more experience of that type of retailing than many of the managers and staff of the larger outlets.
- His opening hours would be much longer and therefore he would sell more.
- He would be able to supervise his small staff, of two or three people, more closely than the manager of a larger outlet.
- Unlike many managers in his type of retailing, he was an excellent salesman, quickly establishing an understanding with customers. Despite his flair for persuading them to buy more than they had intended when they came into the shop (by suggesting they buy products that were related to the original purchase), he remained popular and customers tended to return, even years later, to buy again. This could be a great asset for the supplier.
- With low overheads – because there were no head office costs to absorb and because he did not have a high street site – he could offer more attractive prices than the larger competitors. As his products and those of his competitors were all internationally known brands, his offer of better value for money was genuine and did not derive from offering cheaper substitutes of doubtful quality. His sales prospects were very good if he could have access to the better discounts.

The sales people usually began by taking refuge behind their companies and saying that discounts could only be offered for volume purchases, as a matter of policy. However, the customer knew that they were under pressure to sell volume and he continued to stress how much he expected to sell. In their different ways the sales people began to relent and find different ways of helping – such as: 'Well, we do have some money for promotional offers so we could help you there.' Within two years, this small independent was outselling the branches of some multiples, despite having only a tenth of the selling space.

Many businesses, that make repeated purchases such as the car parts trader, can change their suppliers' printed terms of trade at regular reviews, which are essentially negotiating occasions. Just as there is a natural tendency amongst many people to accept the same suppliers because it is a convenient habit, so it can become habitual to continue with the same terms of trade. Such reviews, which can take place annually for example, are also useful because they demonstrate that the buyer values the supplier's service. Thus the occasion can be used to strengthen trading relationships, even though negotiation takes place. Potentially, this kind of negotiation can be easier to handle because of complex trading relationships on the supplier's side. The buyer can deal with a sales person, the order processing office, the warehouse and the accounts office which issues the invoices. Some of these may have been less than satisfactory on some occasions during the year but it is probable that the sales person who deals with the negotiations did not hear of all of these occasions. This gives the buyer the opportunity to surprise the other party from time to time.

When preparing for this kind of negotiation, the same principles apply as for a single purchase, beginning with the listing of points that can be used in the process of give and take. With repeat-purchase situations, the emphasis is more likely to be on

- delivery, or collection,
- volume rebates,
- credit periods,
- quantity of credit allowed,
- discounts,
- lead time between order and delivery,
- quality of product or service,
- response to complaints.

Negotiating sales

This chapter has described negotiating in some detail mainly from the buyer's point of view, because generally speaking buyers are in the stronger position where there is a ready supply of the item in question.

For the sales person, negotiating is the mirror image of negotiating as buyer. The basic techniques are the same: listing what is wanted and what can be used to deflate the other side's arguments (with the finesse that has been described). Two qualities in the sales person's approach are, however, much more important:

1 A strategic appreciation – to reiterate, deliberately seeking more customers than are required. One company employed sales people

on a commission only basis, the commission varying according to the total value of sales and the profit margins derived. They did not publish fixed prices and sales people were expected to negotiate. Contracts, for specialist office equipment, were usually in excess of £3000. The top salesman was noted for his relaxed and amiable manner. If his schedule of appointments allowed, he took the day off to pursue his favourite sport – fishing. He was once asked why he was so successful and he replied: 'Because I never spend too much time with my friends.' His meaning was that once he had established a good relationship with a customer, he should not linger over it but move on and meet some strangers because they would provide the bulk of his income in the next few months. His strategy protected him personally from many of the threats of a fluctuating market.

One sales director displayed this strategic perception very well. He met with one of his largest customers, who pointed out that they must be the biggest customer he had, probably accounting for 10 per cent of his turnover and should they not have a bigger discount? Calmly the sales director withdrew a notebook from his pocket, consulted it and explained that they were in fact the third largest customer with 0.15 per cent of his sales. The buyer's negotiating posture collapsed and there was no more talk of extra discounts.

2 A cool nerve, so that concessions are never made unless they are traded for counter-concessions. A price reduction is conceded in return for a delayed delivery, for example. To keep one's head under pressure from confident buyers, implying that they can easily go elsewhere, takes a strong belief in the worth of one's business and products.

Coping with the buyer as expert negotiator

The most frequent danger to the negotiating sales person comes from the calm buyer who asks for a detailed breakdown of components of the price, if he does not already have it in the form of a list of separately priced goods, e.g. grocery products. He then takes each component and uses it to negotiate concessions. For example, an office manager, arranging a contract to modernize the electrical wiring of a group of offices, might ask for each different piece of material and each different task to be itemized so that he can try and suggest reasons for reducing the price of each item and thus make a much bigger overall reduction. If he is pressed hard on tangible items like products, the sales person should use the less tangible element of the sale, the service aspects, perhaps the reliability of order processing (orders given over the telephone are always recorded accurately) or the careful handling of the products by delivery truck drivers. If he knows what the customer company wants from him, then he is better placed to use it to sell. These intangibles may well be as important to some of the buyer's colleagues as the prices of many of the products on the order.

Key points

- Only engage in major 'sit down' negotiations if they are important to the business.
- Defeat intimidation by sticking to what you are there for.
- Use rehearsals with a colleague or friend.
- Write down the main lessons of each negotiation, before they are forgotten.

Appendix: Where to get help

First of all make sure that you have extracted value from this book, in the manner suggested in the introduction, by noting those ideas and suggestions that can be helpful to your business. There is no benefit in taking notes for the sake of it, so concentrate on ideas that are suggested in the book and ideas that occur while reading about someone else's business, not necessarily those that are similar to your own.

Useful organizations

The following are some organizations that can help small businesses in the United Kingdom.

- Small business units in Polytechnics and Colleges of Higher or Further Education. These can be found in telephone directories.
- Enterprise Agencies, some of which have clubs for small business people to meet and share problems. Information on the name and whereabouts of your nearest enterprise agency can be obtained from

  Business in the Community
  227A City Road
  London EC1V 1LX
  Tel: 071 253 3716

- Chambers of Commerce, most of whose members have small businesses. Local chambers mainly provide a means of meeting but the big city chambers, like London, provide low-cost advisory facilities for members. Full information on Chambers of Commerce is kept by

  Association of British Chambers of Commerce
  212 Shaftesbury Avenue
  London WC2H 8EW
  Tel: 071 240 5831

For the benefit of small businesses, the Department of Trade and Industry maintains a range of services, which change quite frequently. For up-to-date information, telephone the Department's main office in London (071 215 7877).

The primary training institution for buying is

Institute of Purchasing and Supply
Easton House
Easton on the Hill
Stamford
Lincolnshire PE9 3NZ
Tel: 0780 56777

This Institute also runs the Institute of Credit Management.

The primary training institution for selling is

Chartered Institute of Marketing
Moor Hall
Cookham
Nr Maidenhead
Berks SL6 9QH
Tel: 06285 24922

This Institute also maintains a register of marketing consultants, including sales training consultants.

Apart from contacting these various bodies from time to time, some help can be provided on a do-it-yourself basis, by applying auditing techniques to buying and selling. Just as an accountant from a large practice will have a check-list of questions to apply during a client audit, so the principle can be applied to buying and selling. The check-lists given below have been kept deliberately short, so that they can be used frequently. Probably the best plan is to use each one once a year, both at times well apart from the audit of the accounts.

Buying audit

- In the past month, have any reductions been achieved in the unit prices of any products or services we buy regularly?
- Are we satisfied that no payment is made to any supplier, without checking that the goods or services have been received and that the amount paid is accurate?
- Do we ensure that full advantage is taken of any periods of credit allowed?
- Are our supplier records kept in a manner that makes them easy to use?
- Do we still have a reserve list of potential suppliers for our main products or services?
- Have there been any recent cases of inconveniently late deliveries and have they been resolved, by either complaint to the supplier or removing that supplier from our list of suppliers?
- Could we reduce our stocks?

- With how many of our major suppliers do we attempt to negotiate prices and terms, rather than just accept what they prescribe?
- Are we buying anything we could do without?
- Could we change any of our purchases for alternatives that would be cheaper but still of sufficient quality?

Sales audit

- Do we have more customers than a year ago or less?
- Does each spend more or less than a year ago?
- Who are our main competitors?
- Are they gaining on us or losing?
- Is our selling as good as it could be?
- Have our unique selling points changed in the last year?
- Is our selling as well supported as it needs to be with advertising and other forms of promotion?
- Are there any products or services we could discontinue selling, without loss of profit?
- Are we introducing successful new products as often as our competitors?
- Are we collecting from our customers successfully or are overdues and bad debts increasing?

Glossary

accessory products Products which can easily be sold in association with a major product; for example, distilled water at a car battery shop.

advertising Communicating a message through media such as newspapers or television.

after-sales service Providing the customer with a service after the sale has been completed, for example car servicing.

agent A person or a firm, which sells goods or services on behalf of another person or firm. The usual arrangement is that payment is made by means of a commission, often based on a percentage of sale price.

area samples A marketing research term used when sampling is confined to a particular geographical area.

assembly The process of fastening components together into a single product or part of a single product.

assigned Obligations and benefits under a contract can be assigned to a third party, usually when both the original parties to a contract agree.

bargain A term often used to describe an agreement between two negotiating parties.

batch A method of carrying out a series of similar tasks, one after the other, so that increasing familiarity with the detail reduces the total time required.

blanket contract A type of contract which allows the buyer to request part delivery by the supplier, when circumstances make it appropriate.

bonuses These are often used as extra payments to sales people, individually or as a group, for sales achievement against target.

bought ledger An accounting record, in which a firm's purchases are entered.

brand name An easily remembered term, not descriptive of a product, used to convey its desirable qualities.

bureaucracy An administrative system, in either the private or public sector, in which following all the rules becomes more important than achieving the results for which the system was originally designed.

business options Frequently, there are options or alternatives open to a business, such as which products to stock or what services to provide.

business plan A comprehensive financial plan for a business, often with explanations as to how the various figures were calculated. Business plans are usually required by banks approached to provide finance for new businesses.

business policy This describes the general way in which a firm conducts its business, for example an office services firm which decides to offer only black and white photocopying.

business rates Taxes, levied on many businesses in the United Kingdom, on the basis of property values.

buyers People who actually take decisions to buy.

buying criteria The requirements drawn up in advance before any buying decision is taken.

call frequency The frequency with which a sales person calls on a certain type of customer. Usually the bigger the orders the more frequent the call.

calling off A process of ordering part deliveries against a blanket contract.

capital equipment Usually expensive but necessary and durable equipment, which is operated to recover its cost to the business over a period of time, often years.

case law Law derived from decisions by the courts.

cash and carry A facility, particularly in the grocery trade, which allows traders to collect goods without prior arrangement, on condition immediate payment is offered.

cash flows The movement of money in and out of a business, to be distinguished from profitability, which takes account of outstanding payments due to and by a business. It is possible for a business to be very profitable but have no money because its customers are slow payers, or because it has spent heavily on capital equipment, such as factory or workshop machinery.

catalogues Brochures, books or booklets, listing the goods and/or services for sale.

commission Payment to a sales person, in accordance with his or her personal results, usually as a percentage of sales revenue.

comparison shopping Visiting and perhaps buying from competitors, to make comparisons of value for money.

competitive advantage The aspects of a business which are likely to appeal, more than those of its competitors, to its customers and the ultimate users of its products or services.

components Parts bought in for inclusion in the products manufactured by a firm.

concessions Deliberate offer of benefits, during negotiation, in the expectation that the other party will offer equivalent or greater benefits in return.

consumer The actual user of the product.

contract It can be written, spoken or just implied by behaviour and defines the legal basis for an agreement to buy and sell.

cost plus A term used when the price is determined by costs and a margin for profit.

credit The supply of goods and services with arrangements for payment at a later date.

credit note It signifies the cancellation of the whole or part of an amount due, for the supply of goods and services.

CTN Confectioner, tobacconist and newsagent.

customer The person or firm to whom the sale is made. Sometimes he or she (if it is a person) will be the ultimate user, or consumer, sometimes not.

dealership Usually, a business which specializes in certain products and provides comprehensive facilities, in the way of pre- and after-sales support and technical service.

delivery note A document accompanying delivered goods which describes what they are.

delivery point The place to which the goods are delivered.

devil's advocate Someone who argues the case for the other party, so that it can be fully explored in discussion, for example before the negotiation of a major contract.

direct mail Sending mail direct to a present, past or potential customer.

directories Records, found most frequently in the reference sections of public libraries, with listing usually alphabetical, of either the general public or specialist individuals, such as doctors, or firms, etc.

discount An amount deducted from payment due, usually as an incentive to buy.

distributor A trader who buys goods for resale.

economic purchasing quantities Quantities that are sufficient to achieve lower cost prices but not too high to cause storage inconvenience or incur excessive financing costs.

farmer co-operatives Groups of farmers, who have pooled resources on the basis of one shareholder (not one share), one vote.

financing costs Interest and bank charges paid on funds borrowed for a purchase.

fresh produce Agricultural primary produce, unprotected by chilling or freezing.

goods received sheet Confirmation of receipt to those responsible for checking invoices and arranging payment.

gross margin The profit derived from a sale, after taking account of costs directly related to the product but not overheads.

guesstimates Estimates of future outcomes based on judgement rather than calculation.

hire purchase Taking immediate possession of goods but paying by stages, so that they are first hired and later owned.

hiring This term is usually applied to short-term borrowing, for a fee, of goods such as motor vehicles.

influencers People who influence a purchasing decision but do not actually make it.

intangible assets Aspects of a business, such as customer goodwill, which cannot be seen but nevertheless affect income.

investment return The money that remains, often expressed as a percentage, when the original cost plus interest have been recovered.

invoice A written statement, by the seller, of the buyer's debt.

jobbing engineering workshops Similar to the jobbing printer, only in the engineering business.

jobbing printer A printer who meets a variety of orders from customers, rather than seeking to establish his own range of products, such as books or newspapers.

labour time Time taken by people working on the product/task.

lead time The time that passes between two events, usually the order for a product and its delivery.

leasing Having the use of an asset, on payment of contract fees, for a fixed period of time, usually years or possibly months but not weeks.

letterheads Paper for a firm's correspondence with address and other details shown at the head or the foot.

lock-up garage (or shop) Separate from living accommodation.

mailshot The despatch of a number of similar letters to planned addressees.

maintenance Tasks carried out on machinery, buildings and other equipment, to increase their reliability and durability.

market A defined demand for a product or a service.

marketing research Obtaining information on markets and the manner in which they are approached by suppliers.

media Organs, such as radio stations and television companies, which permit the transmission of advertising messages, news and feature items.

merchandising Displaying goods at the point of sale to encourage purchase.

negotiator One who trades concessions, in the expectation of obtaining benefits superior to those obtained by the other party.

net margin Profit after the deduction of product and overhead costs.

new product development The continuous process of reviewing which products should be removed from the market and which new ones introduced. In manufacturing businesses, it also includes developing and altering the products as better understanding of market demand is achieved.

news bite A summary of the information of greatest interest to the media, which is delivered in such a way as to allow it to be used, in the same form, in a news programme or paper.

objections Overcoming objections is a key sales skill, which demands preparation practice and experience.

offer and acceptance The essentials of any contract.

opportunities Used to indicate opportunities to develop a business, not previously exploited.

order placers People who operate the mechanics of order placing but do not take buying decisions.

order processing The systematic handling of orders so that customer requirements can be met with minimum difficulty.

overdraft facility An agreement by a bank to provide funds up to a predetermined limit.

overheads Costs, such as buildings or vehicles, that cannot necessarily be apportioned to products.

over trading Taking so many orders that the business lacks the finance to cover the costs of production and delivery, before payment is received for the delivered goods.

part deliveries Sending part of an order, rather than waiting for all products to be ready.

percentage mark-up Determining the selling price by adding a percentage to costs.

perceptions of value What the buyer or user perceives as beneficial in the product or service will determine whether or not there is a sale, not what the seller thinks, however rational or well informed he or she may be.

performance What happens in reality, as compared with prediction.

physical assets Things that can be measured, of definite value, which are owned by the business.

pilot Testing a marketing research questionnaire on a few people, to see if it yields the required information with the degree of ease that was anticipated when the exercise was planned.

planning permission This is required by many countries before new structures can be erected or existing ones altered significantly.

procurement The whole process of obtaining goods and services, from initial inquiry to delivery and incorporation in the customer's operations.

product This term can be used to describe not just the product's physical attributes but its other less tangible virtues that may appeal to customers.

product lines These can include a number of different sizes and other variations of a product.

progress chasing Investigating why a supplier has not delivered on time, or alternatively, checking to ensure that the delivery will be as planned.

promotion A very large subject, including every means used to 'push' the product towards the user. These can include sales people, advertising, direct mail and many others.

promotional literature Brochures, leaflets, etc.

prompts Used in marketing research to remind interviewees of possible answers to a question.

prospects A sales person's potential customers.

public relations Obtaining influential third party approval of a product, service or business and communicating that approval to those it is wished to influence.

quantify To express past, present or future situations in numerate as well as verbal terms.

quotation This defines details of the proposed sale, usually goods and services to be provided. Often represents an estimate rather than a commitment.

random samples A term used in marketing research, where each of a number of units or people has an equal chance of being chosen, when a proportion (or sample) is being selected.

ranges A term applied to ranges of products. A trader needs to sell the range of products that his customers expect. For example, a grocer that failed to sell cheese would experience reduced sales for all products.

rebate A repayment of part of the sale price by the seller, usually when the buyer's purchases exceed a predetermined amount.

recommenders People who recommend purchases but do not actually take the decisions.

remuneration Pay and all the other monetary and non-monetary benefits that an employee may receive.

repeat buying Reordering, or returning to buy again, products or services previously bought. In some businesses, such as food retailing, the frequency with which the main items are repurchased, by the same customers, is very important.

replenishment Repurchasing to raise stock to previous levels.

reserve suppliers Suppliers not presently used but considered to be of sufficient quality to be used, if one of the present suppliers proves unsatisfactory.

retailing Selling direct to the consuming public.

sale or return A device used in some industries, to encourage people to try the product, in the belief that many will not return them.

sales control Using a system of reports so that owners or managers can keep in touch with what sales staff are doing and direct their efforts if need be.

sales forecast This is used because it is easier to make corrections – to financial arrangements for example – if some estimate has been made rather than none at all.

sales income Income that only derives from sales of products or services, not from rents for otherwise unused properties, for instance.

sales productivity This is measured in sales per day and influenced by number of calls, potential of customers, skill level of selling.

sales promotion Using incentives to buy, such as subsidized holidays for those successful in a competition, in order to increase sales.

sales reporting Information required daily, including who was visited and with what result.

sales support This includes office support, telephone selling.

samples Samples of product can be distributed to encourage interest and purchase.

sampling A statistical technique whereby only a small proportion of those about whom information is required need to be questioned, to obtain an accurate result.

segment Part of a market which is particular in one or more important respects, such as the age or sex of its people.

service A frequently intangible element, which can help sell any product. For example, assistants in a bookshop who have read either the books themselves or reviews of them.

service levels A means of specifying quality of service. A 24-hour plumbing service is better than next day.

sole trader Not a partnership or a limited liability company.

specifying Describing in precise detail, the purchase(s) that are required.

sponsorship A means whereby events, teams or individuals receive funds from commercial companies, in return for publicity for commercial products or services.

standardization Using the same components in a variety of manufacturing or marketing situations (for example international television advertising).

statute law Law created by a legislature.

stock control Achieving a balance between avoiding out-of-stock situations and having too much in stock.

stockholding costs This can include paying interest on the money borrowed to buy the stock. It may also include paying out more wages because stockholding needs more people if there is more stock.

strategy Using your main resources to achieve a particular result, for example opening a second warehouse to attract more customers.

stratified samples Samples selected at random from various strata or sections of the main population which is being studied.

strengths The qualities of a business which compare favourably with those of competitors.

subassemblies Components fastened together into part products, prior to completing the assembly process.

subcontractor A business which assists another business to fulfil contractual obligations.

supplier development The process of getting to know a supplier so as to make the best use of its particular talents.

supplier performance assessment Comparing a supplier against a measured predetermined standard.

system A sequence of closely related activities, converting known inputs into predictable results.

systematic samples A technique used to simplify sampling, for example stopping at every twelfth house.

targets Quantified achievement levels (for example sales of 2000 units) to aim at.

technical support This is used to help sales staff sell technical products and, often, to provide service for already supplied products.

test market Using a small proportion of the market to predict actual demand in the whole market.

threats Activities or events outside a business, which might bring an end to its current levels of prosperity.

trade paper A journal published regularly for members of a particular trade.

trading Making money by buying and selling.

transaction A single purchase or a series of purchases, made at the same place at the same time.

unique selling point Those aspects which can show a business as better than any of its competitors.

utilities Gas, electricity, telephones, etc.

value analysis Looking at each component of a product and deciding whether it is necessary and, if it is, whether it could be redesigned to cost less.

verification The task of checking incoming invoices and deciding whether they should be paid.

weaknesses Characteristics of a business that compare unfavourably with competitors.

wholesaling Selling for resale.

working capital Capital used to pay the bills that have to be paid before sales revenue comes in. For example wages have to be paid when due but customers may not pay for 30 days, or more.

yardstick An easily understood means of measuring progress.

zero option The option of not doing it at all.

Barclays Guides for the Small Business

The following titles are available in this series:

Wilson: *Financial Management for the Small Business* 0 631 17254 8 ☐
Rogers: *Marketing for the Small Business* 0 631 17247 5 ☐
Aziz: *Computing for the Small Business* 0 631 17256 4 ☐
Wilson: *International Trade for the Small Business* 0 631 17252 1 ☐
Maitland: *Managing Staff for the Small Business* 0 631 17482 6 ☐
Lloyd: *Law for the Small Business* 0 631 17349 8 ☐
Stanworth & Smith: *Franchising for the Small Business* 0 631 17498 2 ☐
Gray: *Managing Growth in the Small Business* 0 631 17249 1 ☐
Gammon: *Buying and Selling for the Small Business* 0 631 17528 8 ☐
All titles are £6.95 each.

You can order through your local bookseller or, in case of difficulty, direct from the publisher using this order form. Please indicate the quantity of books you require in the boxes above and complete the details form below. The publisher will be pleased to negotiate a discount for orders of more than 20 copies of one title.

Payment
Please add £2.50 to payment to cover p&p.

☐ Please charge my Mastercard/Visa/American Express account
card number ☐☐☐☐☐☐☐☐☐☐☐☐☐☐☐☐

Expiry date ____________________
Signature ____________________
(credit card orders must be signed to be valid)

☐ I enclose a cheque for £______ made payable to **Marston Book Services Ltd**

(PLEASE PRINT)
Name ____________________
Address ____________________
____
____________________ Postcode ____________
Tel No ____________________
Signature ____________________ Date ____________

Please return the completed form with remittance to:
Department DM, Basil Blackwell Ltd
108 Cowley Road, Oxford OX4 1JF, UK
or telephone your credit card order on 0865 791155.

Goods will be despatched within 14 days of receipt of order. Data supplied may be used to inform you about other Basil Blackwell publications in relevant fields.
Registered in England No. 180277 Basil Blackwell Ltd.